Praise for *God's Gift of Tremendous Power*

Ann Shakespeare generously shares with the reader the fruit of her own life and prayer experience. With a two-eyed vision she brings into a vivid focus the scientific knowledge of the "quantum field" (the subatomic dynamics of creation) with a dynamic faith in Christ as Creator, Redeemer, and Ascended Lord who "fills all things everywhere." This a vision that can transform both the perception and experience of life in Christ.

Ann's writing is concise, logical, and practical. It is built upon a firm scriptural foundation allied to personal and pastoral experience. It will certainly fulfill its main purpose: to enable individuals to have a transforming encounter with Christ and partake in a new ministry of prayer through the power of the Love of God in Christ.

—The Reverend Canon Andrew Hawes, SSC,
Canon of Lincoln Cathedral with
a particular ministry in spiritual direction
and retreat work

I was utterly enthralled reading this wonderful book, which explains Jesus Christ's "tremendous power" working in and through the whole of creation. The book is richly imbued with God's Word and is deeply spiritual and prayerful.

Ann Shakespeare highlights the central themes of God's love, the Spirit of the risen Jesus Christ, and the need to eschew worldly power and embrace our own weakness. She explains how together they form a prism through which God's all-embracing love can be channelled through us into the world. I also felt that the emphasis she places upon the transformative power of contemplation, prayer, and praying for healing through God's Word is deeply compelling. Through contemplation and prayer we respond to God's call to *"put on the mind of Christ,"* and so pour out His love into the world. This inspirational book gives profound insight into Revelation 21:5, *"See, I am making all things new."*

—**The Reverend Dr. Lynda Pugh, Priest and Spiritual Director in the Diocese of Chester**

GOD'S
GIFT OF
TREMENDOUS
POWER

GOD'S
GIFT OF
TREMENDOUS
POWER

By
ANN SHAKESPEARE

For my husband, Nicholas

Contents

Contents

Preface

I HAVE ASKED NEVILLE JAYAWEERA TO WRITE the foreword to my book because we worked together as colleagues for several years; during that time his teachings and writings have made a profound and lasting impact upon me. They caused me to start discovering the power of the Christ in a way that completely transformed my life and understanding of the Christian faith.

It was Neville's writings that opened to me the deeper things of Christ and introduced me to Bible-based meditation, mysticism, and to the deep truths found in Buddhism and Hinduism. They enabled me to come out of my formal Anglican cocoon and discover a way of life in Christ which is not impeded by a given denominational view.

As a result, my worship and appreciation of the centrality of the Father, the Son, and the Holy Spirit for my salvation has grown, so that today my life in Christ is the most inclusive experience conceivable.

I first met Neville in the 1980s when we were both working for the World Association for Christian Communication (WACC), an international organisation that builds

upon communication rights in order to promote social justice among people of all faiths and cultures. I was editor of
the association's journal, and Neville was a senior director.

At the WACC I was deeply inspired by Neville's rare
grasp of spiritual disciplines and of the doctrines of different
faiths and philosophies. He opened to me the teachings of
the Buddha and the writings of the Hindu Vedanta, among
others, in a way that caused me to see the incarnation, death,
and resurrection of the Christ within a new and profound
perspective. He has written copiously in these areas, and his
writings are freely accessible on his website www.from-the-
unreal-to-the-real.com.

I myself have been shown the way by drinking deeply
from Neville's collection of writings, and what follows
springs from that well. However, I must emphasize that
mine is only a very limited draught; if anyone would like to
drink more deeply, I would urge them to visit his website.

Neville was born into a Buddhist family in Sri Lanka
(then Ceylon) in 1930 and was educated at two of Ceylon's eminent Anglican and Roman Catholic colleges. He
originally planned to study and to practice law, but a strong
inner yearning for truth and meaning—which, years later,
he recognized as the call of the Holy Spirit—caused him to
do a 180-degree turnaround and take an honors degree in
Philosophy instead.

For the first forty years of his life Neville lived as a dedi-
cated Buddhist, studying Theravada Buddhism under the

chief priest of a famous Buddhist teaching institution. Theravada is the name for the school of Buddhism that draws its doctrinal inspiration from writings that are generally accepted as being the oldest record of Gautama Buddha's teachings.

After his period at Ceylon University, Neville was recruited to the elite Ceylon Civil Service, within which he rose rapidly. By the age of forty he had reached the top rung of the service, to become the chairman and director general of the Broadcasting Corporation and special media consultant to the prime minister, Dudley Senanayake.

Soon after that, Neville had a spiritual encounter that caused him to reevaluate his life completely. At the age of forty-two he had an overwhelming experience of the Christ, and for the rest of his life he remained a committed follower of the Christ and a student of truth as expounded in the Bible. Neville says that he does not like to talk at length about this experience because it is inherently inexpressible in words. He quotes Ludwig Wittgenstein, his favorite teacher of philosophy: "Whereof one cannot speak, thereof one must remain silent." However, Neville does say that his experience of the Christ was so utterly radical that it overturned his entire perspective on life, caused him to resign his job, leave his country, and totally reorient all his relationships.

In 1974, shortly after he had resigned from government service, the WACC invited Neville to join them as their director of research and planning. In that role, he has written many articles and books on communication issues. These writings—as well as his writings on history, philosophy, multicultural topics, and international affairs—can also be seen on www.from-the-unreal-to-the-real.com. However, it has been Neville's experience of the Christ that has sustained and illuminated his writings until today (2018).

While concentrating on this experience through prayer and meditation, and writing about his spiritual experiences in depth, Neville was invited by his government to serve in a diplomat's role as well. He accepted an appointment as Sri Lanka's ambassador to the Scandinavian countries—Sweden, Norway, Denmark, and Finland. His role was primarily to fight off the attempt by several European countries to put Sri Lanka on trial. Having completed the assignment successfully, Neville relinquished his position as ambassador and returned to a life of teaching meditation and spirituality to whoever sought him. It was my privilege to be taught by Neville at that time.

One of the most powerful—and practical—revelations came through his teaching on the discoveries of modern physics that deals with the invisible forces of energy, out of which everything in the universe has been created. These discoveries have led many scientists to conclude that the universe is infinite; and because there cannot be more than one infinity, Neville concludes logically that the infinite Christ and the universe must be *one*. Nothing is outside the Christ—absolutely nothing. "Christ is all, and is in all"

(Col. 3:11, NIV), and "in Him all things consist" (Col. 1: 17). Every molecule, atom, and subatomic particle is subsumed in Christ because everything is subject to Him—"He has the power to bring everything under his control," Phil. 3:21, NIRV)—and is resurrected in Him.

If the body of Christ is infinite, and the universe is also infinite, it must follow that the basic fabric of the entire universe is really the body of Christ, because there cannot be two infinite entities.

These things I have learned through Neville's writings, and they have given me a completely new perspective on life and on what it means to be a follower of the Christ. They shed penetrating light on what it means to be "born again" (John 3:3) and to live our lives "hidden with Christ in God" (Col. 3:3). The central truth of Christianity is that the Christ is not concerned with merely making us "better people," but with completely obliterating the old Adamic order and ushering in the New Creation. "Behold, I make all things new" (Rev. 21:5).

Ann Shakespeare

Foreword

by Neville Jayaweera

"Behold! I have given you authority and power."
— Luke 10:19, AMPC

IN HER BOOK, ANN SHAKESPEARE ADDRESSES the concept of power as presented in the Bible.

The first thing that strikes me is that the power she is describing is the power of the Christ—the power that is eternal, uncaused, and not subject to decay or corruption.

The power of the Christ also abides in the Word. "In the beginning was the Word . . . the Word was God. . . . All things were made through Him" (John 1:1, 3), and all things are sustained "by His powerful word" (Heb. 1:3, NIV). Furthermore, the Word is "living and powerful, and sharper than any two-edged sword" (Heb. 4:12); it "lives and abides forever" (1 Pet. 1:23).

Opposed to that Christ power, and completely different in nature, is the power of the world—the power that is perceived by the five senses and always subject to decay and corruption.

What is also unique about Ann's understanding of power is that it is intertwined with her understanding of the basic fabric of the universe (which, in this book, she calls the quantum field), from which everything in existence is made. Whoever has real power—that is, the power referred to in Luke 10:19 above—also has total, ultimate control over the quantum field. Indeed, God's universe unravels within and through it.

The quantum field is an invisible blanket of molecules, atoms, and subatomic particles that constitutes the universe, serving also as a medium of communication. It is the blank slab of clay on which the Lord writes, on which the Lord manifests His love.

The word "power" usually implies power over someone, something, some condition, or some situation. It is always "power over." However, Christ demonstrated His infinite "power over" by relinquishing power, and Ann explains this paradox in her book. A further paradox is that Christ did this precisely in order to share His infinite power with those who believe in Him. To these, Jesus imparts authority to exercise power over snakes and scorpions and all the works of the enemy. By that, Jesus meant more than merely literal snakes and scorpions. These creatures were embodiments of evil and a metaphor for the works of the devil; Jesus was passing the power to control them to all those who put their trust in Him.

The question we ask straight away is where that power comes from. The simple answer is that He Himself received that all-consuming, overwhelming power from His Father in heaven. Ann sees that power manifest not only in the creation and movement of the vast and spreading galaxies but equally in the wingbeat of a butterfly and the chirrup of the smallest sparrow. The Father's objective in passing that power on to His Son was to secure His cooperation for raising the kingdom of God on earth. It was not that the Father needed the help of His creatures in order to raise the kingdom—not at all! The Father could raise the kingdom just by sending forth His Word. But He chose to make the kingdom a shared initiative, a joint effort so that everything, both living and nonliving, bore witness to Him.

The power that Jesus imparts does not just happen once, but it is a continuing process; and that is the secret of resurrection power: "Behold, I make all things new" (Rev. 21:5). Jesus is always creating and recreating. His power is not something that runs out like fuel from the tank, but keeps welling up from the depths and is always being renewed. That is the fundamental difference between the power of the world and Jesus' power.

The power of the world is subject to the law of entropy (the second law of thermodynamics) which says that anything left to itself leaks energy, decays, and dies. Nothing—absolutely nothing that is of, or in, the world—is immune from the law of entropy. The Buddha expressed this in his teaching as the law of impermanence (the law of *Anicca*, as he called it). It is at the heart of the Buddha's teaching, and he explains all the sorrow and unhappiness of the world through this law. He says that when we are attached to anything in the world we are attached to something that is passing away, hence the pain and the anguish of the world.

However, anyone who is rooted in the Christ has access to a fountain that never runs dry and that springs up into everlasting life (John 4:14).

There is power in "His name" as well: "at the name of Jesus every knee should bow" (Phil. 2:10). When the Lord's disciples returned to base from their first missionary outing, they reported to Him, "Lord, even the demons are subject to us in Your name" (Luke 10:17)—but they gave the glory to Him.

The power of Jesus works in and through the quantum field—the universal "fabric." All of the Lord's miracles bear testimony to this fact. When He turned water into wine, in this case He was rearranging the molecular structure of the water to produce wine. Every single miracle performed by Jesus, whether turning water into wine, stilling the storm, riding the waves, or raising Lazarus, involved total power over the molecular world, and Jesus showed that power belonged to Him and not to the world.

All the healing work that the Lord performed, whether restoring hearing to the deaf or vision to the blind, worked at the molecular level.

The power of the world is an ephemeral thing, subject to entropy and corruption even while it lasts. On the other hand, the power of Jesus is eternal, from heaven. That was why He said, "All power is given unto me in heaven and in earth" (Matt. 28:18, KJV), and He bestows that same power upon those who believe in Him.

All things on earth are subject to three basic limitations—gravity, space-time, and entropy. Jesus demonstrated that He had overcome them all. That was why He could say, "be of good cheer; I have overcome the world" (John 16:33).

Ultimately, the power of Jesus is the power of love. It is not a material thing, dependent on anything outside Himself. It poured out from within Him, from the Father who dwelt within Him (John 14:10), and He poured out His love as healing to the world.

Introduction

"How tremendous is the power available to
us who believe in God."

— Ephesians 1:19, PHILLIPS

THE LIFE THAT GOD OFFERS US IS CHARACTERISED by a quality of power that exceeds every other power in the universe. It is described in various translations of Ephesians 1:19 as incomparably, immeasurably, and surpassingly great, and this very same power is made available to us so that we can make a significant difference to the world in which we live.

Jesus has asked us to heal the sick, raise the dead, and to be coworkers in ushering in the kingdom of God. He has also said: "Most assuredly, I say to you, he who believes in Me, the works that I do he will do also; and greater works than these he will do" (John 14:12). In saying "Most assuredly," which can also be translated "Truly, truly," Jesus is placing an emphasis that we cannot ignore.

This book aims to look into the nature of the power that God wants to stream through us, in the same way that He streamed it through Jesus to perform miracles during His life and ministry on earth. Jesus exercised complete control over the fabric—so to speak—of the environment in which He was working. Whether He was healing blind eyes, raising Lazarus, calming a storm, or changing water into wine, Jesus was demonstrating His authority over the molecular structures of His environments.

He calls us to go and do likewise. He has given His followers authority to exercise power over that which is not of God. The Amplified Bible expresses Jesus' words in Luke 10:19 this way: "Listen carefully: I have given you authority [that you now possess] to tread on serpents and scorpions, and [the ability to exercise authority] over all the power of the enemy (Satan); and nothing will [in any way] harm you." All this is in order that we may further cooperate with God in ushering in His kingdom.

God created the universe and is, by definition, Lord of all the elements of which it consists. Advances in physics over the past one hundred years have shown that the universe consists not of separate entities as previously thought, but that it is one vast field of energy—for which "fabric" is a good metaphor—which serves as a vehicle not only for life but also for intelligence and for communication.

The book considers the enormous potential of this vast fabric of the universe to convey different forms of intelligence and communication—specifically, faith and prayer. It aims to shed light on Jesus' assurances that all things are possible to those who believe. He said that "if you have faith as a mustard seed, you will say to this mountain, 'Move from here to there,' and it will move; and nothing will be impossible for you" (Matt. 17:20). He was using this metaphor to explain that one who exercises faith has power over the fabric of the universe and can bring forth from it whatever they command, as long as it is in line with God's Word.

Jesus' teachings are available to absolutely everyone. No one needs to be put off by my references to physics or to scientific metaphors. The "fabric" of the universe is simply the medium within which we all live and breathe.

To live in the power of Ephesians 1:19, and to carry out the work that Jesus asks of us, does not mean that we have to be "super-men" and "super-women." On the contrary, "God has chosen the weak things of the world to put to shame the things which are mighty" (1 Cor. 1:27). That is the paradox of the gospel, and the truth that made the towering apostle Paul rejoice in his weaknesses—because he knew that the less he asserted his own strength, the more the power of Christ could work through him.

This book is not a theological or a scientific study, but it is an attempt to explain, scripturally, how to place ourselves in a position to be channels of God's love and to do the works "which God prepared in advance for us to do" (Eph. 2:10, NIV).

Scripture can never be comprehended solely by the rational mind. It is by entering deeply into the gold mine through prayer and meditation—trusting in the protection and guidance of the Holy Spirit—that we find the veins of gold, waiting to be discovered and quickened into life through faith.

May I pray for us all, therefore, the same prayer for revelation and enlightenment that Paul prayed for the Christians in Ephesus. It begins just before (and includes) our text in Ephesians 1:19, the key verse for this book:

> . . . that the God of our Lord Jesus Christ, the Father of glory, may give to you the spirit of wisdom and revelation in the knowledge of Him, the eyes of your understanding being enlightened; that you may know what is the hope of His calling, what are the riches of the glory of His inheritance in the saints, and what is the exceeding greatness of His power toward us who believe, according to the working of His mighty power which He worked in Christ when He raised Him from the dead and seated Him at His right hand in the heavenly places, far above all principality and power and might and dominion, and every name that is named, not only in this age but also in that which is to come (Eph. 1:17–21).

Chapter 1

What Is Power?

You may be feeling anything but powerful as you begin to read this book. Well, that is an excellent place to start.

"Feelings" of power have very little to do with bearing fruit in the Christian life. In fact, they can be a definite hindrance. Real power, the power that heals and transforms lives and communities, streams forth from God. In order to release that kind of power and to see it work, we have only one responsibility—and that is to get out of the way!

But before we dive in and see exactly how we can "get out of the way" and release the power of God into our own lives and into the lives of others, let us look more closely at the meaning of the word "power."

In all instances, power is the ability to move, withhold, suppress, oppress, create, change, uphold, and elevate things at an organic, inorganic, or psychological level. Broadly speaking, there are three kinds of power: material, psychological, and spiritual power. For the purposes of this book, we will concentrate on material and spiritual power.

Everything in existence has its origin in spiritual power: "In the beginning God created the heavens and the earth" (Gen. 1:1). The gospel of John makes it clear that "God is Spirit" (John 4:24). Therefore, we know that the parent force of all creation is spiritual power.

In the beginning, "the earth was without form, and void" (Gen. 1:2). So how did material, or visible, entities come into existence? We find the answer in Hebrews 11:3: "the worlds were framed by the word of God, so that the things which are seen were not made of things which are visible."

God created the universe, the earth, plants, living creatures and human beings by means of commands. He spoke everything into visible existence with His words: "Let the dry land appear" (Gen. 1:9); "Let us make humankind in our image" (Gen. 1:26, NRSV); and so forth.

God needed a canvas, so to speak, through which to express Himself in three-dimensional form. In recent decades, physicists have started to describe this "canvas" in scientific terms, but opinions still vary regarding the scientific definition of the makeup of the canvas (the essential fabric) of the universe. One way of describing it is to say that it is made up of immense swirls, or fields, of vibrating energy which interact and blend with each other. In turn, these fields of energy constitute one vast, universal field of energy which, in this book, I am calling the "quantum field."

I acknowledge that "quantum field" is *not* an exact scientific term, but I am using it as helpful shorthand to describe the basic fabric of the universe without going into complex scientific detail, which is not necessary for the purposes of this book. *Quantum* is originally a Latin word meaning "how much"—relating to size and amount. The word has since come to mean the smallest amount you can have. Therefore, by "quantum field" I am referring to the seamless fabric which comprises the smallest, most fundamental components of the universe.

Another metaphor for quantum field, in addition to "canvas" and "fabric," could be the soft clay from which God sculpted His creation into existence. This "clay," or vital energy, is the basic substance of everything that exists in the universe, including human beings. It is the invisible essence that connects and interconnects us all.

The quantum field (QF) is spread everywhere throughout the universe. It is the fundamental reality in which we live. Everything that we can see, hear, feel, touch, and smell is made from out of the QF. All matter—be it human beings, plants, animals, or inanimate substances—is made up of vibrating energy. The visible is created out of what is invisible.

Faith believes that the quantum field is God's canvas. Scientists do not necessarily agree with that description. However, there is substantial overlap between the Word of God and scientific discovery, and we will be looking at the significance of that overlap later on in this book.

God spun everything out of His quantum field, ranging from the massive, spreading galaxies to the tiniest, most delicate butterfly. What human beings have been able to observe of God's creation is already so vast and complex that it defies description. However, even so, scientists estimate that they have detected barely 4 percent of the universe—leaving a staggering 96 percent still to be discovered and observed.

Psalm 33:6 declares: "By the word of the LORD were the heavens made; and all the host of them by the breath of His mouth." The Hebrew word translated "heavens" here can also be translated "firmament." In these two short phrases lie a demonstration of divine might and intelligence that are utterly beyond comprehension or imagining.

The most significant advances in the study of the universe are relatively recent. It is particularly striking, therefore, that the oldest recorded portion of God's Word—the book of Job—contains some of the most up-to-date and accurate descriptions of the creation of the universe: "He stretches out the north over empty space; He hangs the earth on nothing" (Job 26:7). That fact is repeated in several other places including the book of Isaiah: "He . . . stretches out the heavens like a curtain, and spreads them out like a tent to dwell in" (Isa. 40:22). It is only in the last ninety years that the American astronomer, Edwin Hubble, discovered that the universe has indeed been expanding—or stretching—since it was first created, and that it continues to expand and stretch to this very day.

Then there is the microscopic world, with its countless, breathtaking creations. Take DNA, for example—the genetic code that determines all the characteristics of a living thing and that makes you, you. It serves as an instruction manual in every one of your roughly 30 trillion cells, so that each cell knows how to keep you in working order. If uncoiled, the DNA in all your cells in your body would stretch to the moon and back almost 1,500 times!

DNA is just one expression of the power that assembled and maintains the marvel that is your body, with its 100,000 miles of blood vessels and 30 trillion cells, working together in a complex symphony of interactions.

The power of the Spirit of God is the source of everything. It is the uncaused cause, and therefore it can never be nullified. It is supreme over every other power.

It is all-encompassing in might (omnipotence), in infinity (omnipresence), and in knowledge and wisdom (omniscience).

It is eternal. It is creative, life-giving, and always renewing.

It is righteous and perfect in every respect. It cannot be sullied, violated, or diminished in any way, by any other agent or power.

It is invisible, and yet it manifests in visible ways.

This is the supreme power that created everything.

Every inch of creation reveals wonders that far transcend the ability of the human mind to fully comprehend. The paragraphs above give a small insight into the awesome power of God who is the designer, creator, and sustainer of it all—the God who counts the hairs on our head, and who does not lose sight of the smallest sparrow.

However, whether we are talking of one little sparrow or of a vast galaxy of stars, there is a distinction between the quantum field and the environment within which it operates. We need to ask ourselves: What is the nonmeasurable "something" that imparts power to the quantum field? Faith declares that the essence of that something is Spirit—invisible, intangible, and itself not subject to entropy. That is, it is beyond disease, decay, and death.

It is all too apparent, however, that the quantum field itself is *not* beyond disease, decay, and death. In fact, those are the chief characteristics that ultimately define our existence on earth. They are the results of the Fall—the consequences of our separation from God.

It was the gift—and the exercise—of free will that caused the Fall of humankind and led to all the subsequent, terrible consequences that occur on earth on a daily basis. However, without the gift of free will, human beings would have been like robots, programmed to love. Love, to be love, cannot be programmed—hence, the choice that we were given right from the beginning.

Whether or not the account of Adam and Eve is taken literally, the fact remains that human beings chose to collude with Satan's lies and to turn away from God, to cut off their source of divine life, and therefore become closed systems or broken branches with only a finite supply of sap.

It is indeed as though another power seems to have asserted control now—an evil and destructive one. However, it is vital to hold on to the fact that this destructive power is temporary: "behold, I create new heavens and a new earth: and the former shall not be remembered, nor come into mind" (Isa. 65:17, KJV). Not only is it temporary, but through the death and resurrection of Jesus Christ, God has already provided the resources for His children to start to take back the authority that was forfeited in the garden of Eden and to follow closely in the footsteps of their Master who declares, "Behold, I make all things new. . . . I am the Alpha and the Omega, the Beginning and the End" (Rev. 21:5–6).

It was to destroy destruction—so to speak—that God became incarnate in Jesus Christ: in order to reconcile us to Himself, to impart His Spirit throughout the quantum field, and to empower us to work with Him in ushering in the new creation. It was on our behalf that Jesus Christ died to overcome the power of evil and to enable us to be co-heirs with Him in His resurrection and ascension, with "authorities and powers having been made subject to Him" (1 Pet. 3:22).

The quantum field itself is morally neutral—it is neither good nor bad, but it depends upon the quality of consciousness that controls it. God created it and chose to give it to human beings so that they could have dominion over it and control it: "God blessed them and said to them, 'Be fruitful and increase in number; fill the earth and subdue it'" (Gen. 1:28, NIV). But then came the Fall and the quality of consciousness that remained in control became deeply and tragically flawed.

The question now is: Who or what can enable significant change to happen in our material world and circumstances? Who or what can bridge the invisible and the visible, the intangible and the tangible—and hold them all together under one source of control?

To answer that question, we must refer back to the non-measurable "something" that imparted power to the quantum field in the first place.

That is the Christ. "For God had allowed us to know the secret of his plan, and it is this: he purposes in his sovereign will that all human history shall be consummated in Christ, that everything that exists in Heaven or earth shall find its perfection and fulfilment in him" (Eph. 1:9–10, PHILLIPS).

From the Christ flows the "tremendous power" of Ephesians 1:19. The same power that created the universe, that took on human flesh as Jesus of Nazareth, healed all kinds of diseases, raised the dead, and controlled the elements. The very same power "which He worked in Christ when He raised Him from the dead" and "put all things under His feet" (Eph. 1:20, 22). This is the power of resurrection and renewal.

Now, Christ calls us to cooperate with Him in unifying and renewing God's broken universe, "Not by might nor by power, but by My Spirit" (Zech. 4:6)—by invoking His death and resurrection to bridge the gulf between the material and the spiritual.

That was what Jesus meant when He said, "All power is given unto me in heaven and in earth" (Matt. 28:18, KJV), and "I have given you the power . . . to overcome all the enemy's power" (Luke 10:19, PHILLIPS).

Power to dissolve, configure, and reconfigure. Power to trust, to stand upon and to declare and bring into manifestation the Word of God. The Word that affirms that Jesus destroyed all that is not of God on Calvary, and that He has indeed ushered in a new creation.

A key scripture is "Behold I make all things new" (Rev. 21:5), which means that Christ is reconfiguring the universe according to His will. The apostle Paul points us toward this truth in his letter to the Galatians: "what counts is the new creation" (Gal. 6:15, NIV). Christ appoints us to cooperate with Him in this awesome task. Only, we must abide in Him and let His Word abide in us, and His resurrection power will flow out from us and through us, making all things new.

Chapter 2

Jesus Christ:
A Paradox Like No Other

THE CHRIST—THE ESSENCE OF ALL POWER

IN ORDER TO BANISH ALL TRACE OF SEPARATION, and to restore full relationship with human beings, God entered into a seemingly impossible contradiction, or paradox: He came to earth as both man and as God. What is more, He arrived on earth embodying two equally balanced opposites. He was not just partially man and mostly God. No, He was fully man and fully God. It is to this astounding paradox that we turn in this chapter.

The awesome, incomprehensible power of which we had a tiny glimpse in the first chapter all emanated from God the Father through Christ, who is "the radiance of God's glory and the exact representation of his being" (Heb. 1:3, NIV).

Christ was in the beginning with God, and all things were constituted in Him: "For in him all things were created: things in heaven and on earth, visible and invisible, whether thrones or powers or rulers or authorities; all things have been created through him and for him" (Col. 1:16, NIV). The Christ was, and is, supreme in power, in authority, in righteousness, in purity, in justice, in wisdom, in knowledge, in creativity, and in love. He is described in Scripture as the "only Ruler, the King of kings and Lord of lords" (1 Tim. 6:15, NIV) and as "God, our Savior. . . . All glory, majesty, power, and authority are his before all time, and in the present, and beyond all time!" (Jude 1:25, NLT).

Christ exercises His power in myriad ways at myriad levels, but there are three particular moments in time when His power was manifest in the most supreme ways. The first was (is) the point of creation itself, when the universe and everything in it came into existence. The second was (is) the demolition, on the cross, of the entire fallen world order and everyone and everything in it which was not the handiwork of God. The third was (is) His resurrection from the dead and, simultaneously, the ushering in of a completely new creation, the kingdom of God, which is permeated and governed by the word of the Lord.

It is the power of love that led the Christ—the maker of heaven and earth—to become incarnate as a human being, in order to save humankind and to reconcile the human race back to God the Father.

THE CHRIST—THE ESSENCE OF ALL WEAKNESS

Therein lies the heart of the most staggering of all paradoxes: that the God of all power should lay down every hint of that power and that He should empty Himself out so completely: "Christ . . . did not cling to his prerogatives as God's equal, but stripped himself of all privilege" (Phil. 2:7, PHILLIPS).

Furthermore, Christ willingly subjected Himself to the infinitely inferior "power" of fallen human beings, in order to save His creation and make love perfect once again. Even though Satan—the prince of this world—could wield no power over Jesus because He was sinless; nevertheless, out of loving identification with those He had come to save, Jesus submitted Himself to all the effects of Satan's work since the Fall. He took upon Himself all the evil and darkness that had accumulated through generation after generation over thousands of years—as well as the evil that continues to accumulate. Christ has absorbed, and is absorbing, everything that is not of God into Himself. He did this to set us free from the bondage of this inescapable cycle of sin and its vast, cumulative network of terrible consequences.

He had a second, astonishing reason for doing it, and that was to enable us—through His own utter weakness—to enter into the "tremendous power" of Ephesians 1:19.

Much is preached and taught about the fact that Jesus died to save us from our sins and to enable us to enter eternal life. That is already a glorious gift. But let us not stop there. Let us press forward to believe and to appropriate the Word of God, which teaches us that we are empowered by God in order to bear lasting fruit.

It is tragic that very little is preached about this gift of tremendous power, which God makes available to every believer who would open their heart to receive it. Before looking further into this gift, it should have even greater meaning and impact if we recall the steps taken by God to restore relationship with His children and to entrust us with a power that is beyond imagining.

It is indeed wondrous that omnipresent God, who is Spirit (John 4:24), should limit Himself within the form of a tiny baby, making Himself completely dependent upon fallen human beings for all His needs at the start of His life on earth.

Weakness—or non-power—was the distinguishing mark of Jesus' entire life on earth. It is striking that the only occasions he used power were to help others. He never used it for His own benefit. On the contrary, He made Himself vulnerable to the most searing offences, insults, and humiliation from the very first day of His life on earth to His very last.

The King of kings and Lord of lords began His earthly life in a feeding trough that was used to feed animals. The familiar account of the baby Jesus being wrapped in swaddling clothes and laid in a manger tends to dull us to the stark reality of those early days of His incarnation. Whether the feeding trough was actually in a stable, or whether it was in a covered shelter in a house where animals were taken in on cold nights . . . it doesn't really matter. The fact is that it would not have been a clean and pleasant place to sleep. Animal feces are extremely strong-smelling, especially in an enclosed space, and the area surrounding the trough is likely to have been very dirty indeed.

Lying there in a feeding trough, God was not only identifying with refugees, outcasts and those in dire poverty. The feeding trough also spoke volumes about Jesus' future calling, which was to give His own body and His own blood in order to feed His people—to be our Bread of Life.

As an adult, Jesus constantly made Himself vulnerable to hate and rejection. Perhaps especially shocking is that it even happened in His hometown of Nazareth.

It is no minor thing that His former townspeople—most of whom are likely to have known Jesus personally because Nazareth was small—did not stop to give Him the benefit of the doubt and to talk calmly with Him. On the contrary, they rejected Him out of hand, thrust Him out of Nazareth, and attempted to kill their former townsman by throwing Him over the brow of a cliff.

Jesus could reasonably have exercised supernatural power in Nazareth in a positive way—by healing people and performing miracles—in order to assert His dignity, assuage His hurt, and to try to gain His former neighbors' respect. However, the measure of His self-emptying love is demonstrated in a most extraordinary way here. Instead of drawing on the supernatural power that was constantly available to Him, the King of kings chose to humble Himself under the consciousness of the people of Nazareth—for love does not force faith: "He did not do many mighty works there because of their unbelief" (Matt. 13:58).

Elsewhere, our God was accused of having a demon (John 8:48–52) and of drawing His power from Satan (Matthew 12:24), when He was teaching in the temple in Jerusalem. At those very moments, Jesus could have wiped the earth clean of demons and humanity alike—in a fraction of a second. But stunningly, in the cause of love, He chose instead to stand in absolute humility and respect, in the company of His mocking accusers, continuing to talk with them. Likewise, when they took up stones to hurl at Him, He could have called on His spiritual power to dematerialise and simply disappear.

But instead, Jesus did something extraordinary and poignant beyond words: He, God, actually hid Himself from human beings. Does that not take us back to the third chapter of Genesis? By hiding, Jesus was taking upon Himself the shame and pain of Adam who had rebelled, and who consequently hid himself, along with his wife, from the presence of the Lord God (Gen. 3:8). The Lord God had called out to Adam and said, "Where *are* you?"

Thousands of years later, hanging in agony on a cross, Jesus returned this same, heartrending call to God His Father: Where are you? "Why have you forsaken Me?" (Matt. 27:46).

On both occasions, the only one crying out for restored relationship was God. He pursues us with unrelenting, inextinguishable Love.

It is worth emphasising here that there is no question of God the Father "punishing" Jesus for the sins of humankind, in order to love us, as some writers have claimed. No. God the Father has always loved us: "God so loved the world" (John 3:16), and His Son incarnated Himself as Jesus Christ in order to remove every single obstacle and to enable full, unhindered communion between Godhead and human beings. God is one, manifesting Himself as three. Scripture makes it clear that in Christ Jesus "dwells all the fullness of the Godhead bodily" (Col. 2:9). There is no hint of separation there.

Then what can be said of the passion and crucifixion? What can be added to the billions of words that have been written, spoken, and sung? For His is the ultimate self-emptying, self-giving, self-annihilating act of love—fulfilled by the same God who set an unfathomable 100 billion galaxies perfectly in place.

Perhaps what can be added is that, to my knowledge, no portrayal of the death of Jesus even comes close to conveying what actually happened in the last hours of His life. Most artwork has sanitized and minimized the sufferings of Jesus, undermining the indescribable truth of what He did—for love of the human race.

So unspeakable was His suffering—physical, mental, and spiritual—that Jesus no longer even looked like a human being: "his appearance was so disfigured beyond that of any human being and his form marred beyond human likeness"

(Isa. 52:14, NIV). In other words, the body of the Lord of lords and King of kings was reduced to an unrecognisable mass of flesh, blood, and bones.

It is for a very specific purpose that we have looked so deeply into these harrowing events of Jesus' life, and it is important to note that these are just a few among the countless tormenting occurrences that assailed Him throughout His entire ministry. The purpose for doing this is for us to see how completely and utterly Jesus laid down His right to His place in the Godhead, even though He was fully God as well as fully man. It is vitally important to see this, for three reasons:

1. To understand the depths to which God chose to go in order to restore full relationship—indeed, full union—with the human race.

2. To see that it was His complete identification with human beings that enabled Jesus to take upon Himself all sin committed from the beginning of humanity, plus all the cumulative effects of sin, as well as the perpetrator of sin in each human being—the "old Adam."

3. To see that in emptying Himself out and, literally, making Himself "nothing" (Phil 2:7, NIV), Jesus modeled for the human race how to live the Christian life—in other words, how to lay down self-interest

and to die to self in order to enter into the abundant life that He promised in John 10:10, the life that expresses the "tremendous power" of Ephesians 1:19.

In chapters 4 to 7, we will look more deeply into what this means, and how we can apply Jesus' teaching to our own lives. But let us first see how Jesus' total self-surrender and emptying-out affected His earthly ministry. It is so important to reflect on this, because there may be a tendency to miss the full significance of the miracles of Jesus by assigning them to the Son of God. *Well, it's easier for Jesus because He was God, wasn't He?* Yes, He was God but He chose to empty Himself completely and to set aside His divinity—and love was His only reason.

We must see that it was *not* the Son of God who performed those miracles. No. It was indeed the Son of Man who healed the multitudes, calmed storms, and raised the dead.

Please do not miss the implications here for us. Jesus told us clearly that if we believe in Him, we will do what He did: "he who believes in Me, the works that I do he will do also; and greater works than these he will do" (John 14:12).

We will come back to this astounding declaration in chapter 5, but it is helpful to note here that in the Gospels Jesus was given two titles: Son of God and Son of Man. By contrast, we believers have one title and one alone. We are called sons and daughters of the Most High God, because—through Christ's work on the cross—we have been born of God and adopted into His family. Sons and daughters of human beings are nowhere to be found after the resurrection of Jesus. In Luke 20:36 (NRSV), Jesus Himself calls us "children of the resurrection."

Paul makes this clear in his letter to the church at Corinth: "if One died for all, then all died. . . . Therefore, from now on, we regard no one according to the flesh. Even though we have known Christ according to the flesh, yet now we know Him thus no longer" (2 Cor. 5:14, 16). This is because, as the last Adam (that is, the last "Son of Man") Jesus completely obliterated the separated, broken-branch Son of Man race upon the cross. Thereafter, "if anyone is in Christ, there is a new creation: everything old has passed away; see, everything has become new!" (2 Cor. 5:17, NRSV).

Jesus' primary purpose in coming to earth was to redeem the human race. The second purpose was the establishment of the kingdom of God on earth, as in heaven—which could not make its entry unless and until every iota of debt had been paid off. That final payment was made upon Calvary.

A further purpose that Jesus accomplished was to demonstrate how to live the fulfilled and empowered life that God intended the human race to live. He modeled for us how to obtain access to the wondrous power that He demonstrated during His life on earth. Jesus sums up the essence of this model in His words: "I can do nothing on my own initiative or authority" (John 5:30, AMP).

What kind of model is this?

It is the model of emptying out the old and powerless . . . in order to make way for the entrance of the new, the glorious, and the tremendously powerful. Jesus points to the very practical results of His self-emptying: "the Father who dwells in Me does the works" (John 14:10). Elsewhere in the gospel of John, Jesus heals a man who had lain ill for thirty-eight years, then He says: "Most assuredly, I say to you, the Son can do nothing of Himself, but what He sees the Father do" (John 5:19).

The point here is that Jesus said that He could do nothing by Himself—no demonstrations of healing, no words of wisdom and encouragement, no power at all to carry out His God-given mission. Therefore, how much more do *we* need to understand that, by ourselves, neither do we have the power to accomplish that which God has called us to do. Realising our weakness and emptiness is a vital step towards gaining access to the power of God.

OUR ACCESS TO THE POWER OF GOD

Ever since the Holy Spirit was spread abroad after the ascension of Jesus Christ, God's power has been based upon the quality of Oneness. Jesus prayed this prayer for all believers before He went to His death: "that they all may be one, as You, Father, are in Me, and I in You; that they also may be one in Us . . . that they may be one just as We are one: I in them, and You in Me" (John 17:21–23).

God's power is fully present and operative in one divine source, and yet it expresses itself in an infinity of manifestations. To the limited human eye those manifestations seem to be separate, but they are not separate. They share one nature, in the same way that water, steam, frost, hail, and ice share the same nature. They look very different, their behaviors are different, and the impacts they make are very different—but their essence is uniform. Without that essential substance, those multiple manifestations could not exist.

At this point, someone might say, "Well, that is the same for human beings. We all look separate, but we are all children of God and are made in His image and likeness—so in essence we are one." Tragically, however, we are not one essence (that is, without faith in the reconciling work of Christ)—we are separated and divided—and that was the Fall of humankind.

God designed us to live in union with Him and with each other; separation was never in His plan. The immediate effects of separation were fear, a focus on self, and a desire to hide from God: "I heard Your voice in the garden, and I was afraid because I was naked; and I hid myself" (Gen. 3:10), said Adam to God.

The account in Genesis reveals that this emergence of fear and self-interest rapidly spawned anger, envy, lying, self-protection, self-justification, hostility, and murder. While separateness, thankfully, does not always lead to murder, our world today is not dissimilar, in behavior and attitudes, to the world described in Genesis 4 onward.

That is why God incarnated Himself in Jesus Christ—to put an end to all separation and division by reconciling us all to Himself through the sacrifice of Jesus Christ on the cross, and through His mighty resurrection and ascension.

It is only by fully identifying ourselves with the death and the resurrection of Jesus Christ that we can find practical, active, and permanent freedom from captivity to separateness.

In the next chapter, we will see how this wondrous gift of freedom is available to anyone who would seek it with all their heart. It is not about mental intelligence or a learned understanding of the Bible. It is about having a gentle and humble longing to experience more of God.

Chapter 3

The Power of Absolute Weakness

IN ORDER TO LIVE IN THE FREEDOM that Christ purchased for us, and to experience His power, there is one key truth that we need to grasp: The greatest power emerges from absolute weakness.

In chapter 2 we saw this truth applied supremely in the life of Jesus. It is awe-inspiring to reflect on how utterly astonishing it is that the omnipotent God embraced the characteristic of weakness. Weakness is not, and has never been, an inherent part of the Godhead. It was for our sakes— for God's love of humanity—that He took upon Himself a *quality of being* which is totally contrary to His holy nature. It was by taking on this quality of being that enabled Him to contravene His character and actually to become weakness on our behalf. He did this for the singular purpose of extinguishing weakness, and all the effects of weakness, for evermore.

It is worth noting that weakness is not the same as *meekness*, which is a fruit of the Holy Spirit meaning gentleness and humility. It is only through drawing on the grace and the power of God that human beings can demonstrate true meekness. By contrast, weakness means lacking strength or power, and it is not a godly quality.

One of the most astounding verses in the whole of Scripture is: "He [God] made Him [Jesus Christ] who knew no sin to be sin for us, that we might become the righteousness of God in Him" (2 Cor. 5:21).

If God did not ordain weakness, how did it come into being?

Weakness became an inherent part of being human as soon as humanity cut itself off from the Source of all power. That was the Fall. Since then, weakness has demonstrated itself in human beings in countless ways, the most fundamental being our inability to prevent our own decay and death. This was the logical consequence of severing our life source—our union with God. We literally became like broken branches, and our lives have reflected that condition to this day. At birth, our bodies contain enough sap to maintain vitality for some years or even several decades, but then the sap starts to dry up and, because we are completely cut off from the parent Tree, there is no way that we can draw upon Its vital sap to replenish our resources. So, progressively, we wither and die.

However, by dying and rising again on our behalf, Jesus Christ has totally reversed that situation. For us, He has transformed weakness into strength that surpasses our imagination.

"For though He was crucified in weakness, yet He lives by the power of God. For we also are weak in Him, but we shall live with Him by the power of God" (2 Cor. 13:4).

How remarkable it is when our eyes fall upon the apostle Paul's triumphant declaration: "when I am weak, then I am strong" (2 Cor. 12:10b). Paul is a towering figure in the New Testament, with an impeccable religious pedigree and elite education. "Weak" was probably the least appropriate description of this man who took on the Roman Empire and ended up "turn[ing] the world upside down" (Acts 17:6).

However, Paul knew that the secret of true power lay in absolute weakness. That is the paradox and the logic of the Cross. He had heard the Lord saying to him: "My grace is sufficient for you, for My strength is made perfect in weakness." Rather than boast in his formidable, personal qualifications, Paul most gladly boasted in his weaknesses, "that the power of Christ may rest upon me" (2 Cor. 12:9).

What was it exactly that Paul had discovered? What was it that caused him to declare with overflowing confidence that he had lost everything for the sake of Christ and that furthermore he considered it all "to be mere rubbish (refuse, dregs)"? (Phil. 3:8, AMPC).

This is an astonishing statement by a man who had described himself only two verses earlier as "a Hebrew of the Hebrews; concerning the law, a Pharisee; concerning zeal, persecuting the church; concerning the righteousness which is in the law, blameless" (Phil. 3:5–6).

It is not known whether Paul had met or seen Jesus Christ in the flesh before His crucifixion, but he certainly had a life-changing encounter with the risen Lord on the Damascus Road. This encounter was not merely subjective; Paul's travelling companions also heard Jesus' voice (Acts 9:7) and saw the great light that fell around Paul (Acts 22:9).

This experience caused Paul to turn his life around completely. Instead of hounding and persecuting Christians and hating their leader, he became a passionate and devoted follower of Jesus Christ, enduring intense persecution for the sake of the gospel.

The all-consuming focus of Paul's life is captured in a letter he wrote to the churches in Galatia: "I have been crucified with Christ; it is no longer I who live, but Christ lives in me" (Gal. 2:20) and "God forbid that I should boast except in the cross of our Lord Jesus Christ, by whom the world has been crucified to me, and I to the world" (Gal. 6:14). Paul knew, beyond a shadow of a doubt, that the source of all true power and love was, and is, exhibited at Calvary.

There is an astounding paradox concerning the power that the apostle Paul promises is available to those who believe. The power that he describes in the letter to the Ephesian church is of "immeasurable and unlimited and surpassing greatness" (Eph. 1:19, AMP). There is no power anywhere that can compete with it, come near it, or overcome it.

Yet—and here is the paradox—the only way for us to access and experience that power is to take the diametrically opposite route. That is, we must not only relinquish all power, at every level of the outer and inner planes of our lives, but also willingly accept the weakest and the lowest state imaginable—and sometimes this may actually be *beyond* imagination.

Another name for this power of all powers is love.

Most astounding of all, however, is that we human beings have freely been given the direction, the means, and the ability to access and live our day-to-day lives in the flow of that immeasurable power.

It is Paul himself who explains so clearly how we can step into that flow of immeasurable power, through understanding and appropriating what Jesus accomplished on our behalf on the cross. His teachings, contained in his letters to the different churches and church leaders, encompass the meaning of Jesus' crucifixion, resurrection, and ascension, and its application to all those who believe and trust in Jesus Christ.

It is to those teachings of Paul that we now turn.

WHO AND WHAT DIED UPON THE CROSS?

Jesus Christ was not the only person to die upon the cross. Other people and other things died with Him—on the same cross.

- The perpetrator and father of all sins, the devil, was destroyed on the cross, as is made clear in Hebrews

2:14: "Inasmuch then as the children have partaken of flesh and blood, He Himself likewise shared in the same, that through death He might destroy him who had the power of death, that is, the devil."

- Every single person who has ever lived, who is living, and who will live has been crucified with Christ on the cross: "if One died for all, then all died" (2 Cor. 5:14). Also crucified were our sins and all the accumulated effects of every sin, from the beginning of time until the end of time.

- The world itself died to believers through the cross (Gal. 6:14), along with all the structures and systems of sin erected by human beings.

- Also crucified with Christ was the "damning evidence of broken laws and commandments which always hung over our heads" (Col. 2:14, PHILLIPS). In other words, all the effects of the law of sin and death (as you sow, so shall you reap) were obliterated on the cross.

The cross was host only to agony, and to death upon death. Even though the sun would have been high in the sky, its light disappeared and darkness covered the land . . . and Jesus died.

At that terrible moment, however, when despair, death, and utter darkness seemed to be the only victors, something very wonderful happened inside the temple of Jerusalem. The thick curtain that guarded the most holy section of the temple, the Holy of Holies—symbolising the very presence of God Himself—was torn apart from top to bottom (Matt. 27:51).

This curtain, woven out of linen, was about sixty feet high, and Jewish tradition estimates that it was about four inches thick. It was impossible for human beings to tear it with their bare hands—and certainly not from the top; it towered sixty feet above them. In any case, no one but the high priest ever entered the Holy of Holies, and that just once a year, on pain of death (Lev. 16:2).

Up to that moment, the purpose of the curtain had been to keep the people permanently separated from God, because God had said, "You cannot see My face; for no man shall see Me, and live" (Exod. 33:20).

The significance of the tearing of this curtain (or thick veil) is truly awe-inspiring. God took upon Himself the killing weight of the accumulated sin of human beings and of the world, and died . . . in order for us to live—and not just to "live," but to live more abundantly than ever before (John 10:10).

It means that at the moment Jesus died, the impenetrable veil of sin that had separated humankind from God since the Fall was torn right open. It means that all people are now completely free to enter into the very presence of God without fear, without condemnation . . . but with love alone.

Not only do we have the right to enter into the very presence of God, but in fact we are told that we are united with the Spirit of God Himself.

Jesus was the first to point toward this truth, in conversation with His disciples just before He was arrested and crucified. He forewarned them that even though the world would shortly not be able to see Him anymore, it would be a very different experience for His disciples. He promised them, "you will know that I am in My Father, and you in Me, and I in you" (John 14:20).

Jesus went on to make one of the most intimate promises in the New Testament: "If anyone loves Me, he will keep My word; and My Father will love him, and We will come to him and make Our home with him" (John 14:23).

It is to this most intimate communion and union with God that we turn, in the next chapter.

Chapter 4

What It Means to Be United with Christ

OUR UNION, OR ONENESS, WITH ALMIGHTY GOD is way beyond the grasp of our natural minds, but it is absolutely vital so let us press into it—and to not give up.

Our minds and bodies may scream: "No! How can I possibly be one with God if I am ill, feel depressed, keep failing, struggle so much with life?" May I urge you to continue doing whatever is needed or helpful at the physical level, and then make a decision to look into the truth of God's Word—to find out what it says about you.

Yes, God's Word speaks volumes about you. If you look into it, you will find that it is an accurate, never-changing mirror, reflecting back to you exactly who you are and to whom you belong: "Don't you realize that your body is the temple of the Holy Spirit, who lives in you and was given to you by God? You do not belong to yourself" (1 Cor. 6:19, NLT). In his letter to the Colossians, Paul describes your identity very succinctly: "you died, and your life is hidden with Christ in God" (Col. 3:3).

The life of Christ is now your life, and all that is true of Christ is true of you. Christ is now your own identity.

It is only as we say "Yes" to this fact, and start to walk in faith in our new identity, that the truth of who we really are will begin to emerge into our experience. It does require that we look into the Scriptures and meditate upon them, taking them into our days and nights, and applying them in our lives. It means resisting the temptation to give up when nothing seems to be happening.

It helps to remember that there is One who is infinitely more desirous that you come to know and experience who you are in Christ than you are—that is your righteous Father; and He gives you a constant supply of the Holy Spirit to teach you, to encourage you and to guide you.

A stumbling block for many is a key verse which actually gives us entry into this new life: "I have been crucified with Christ; it is no longer I who live but Christ lives in me" (Gal. 2:20). We find it extremely difficult to identify with this verse because we are still breathing—clearly not dead. We look at our limitations and failures, and conclude that these cannot be signs of the indwelling Christ. So it remains at the level of theory, very much a mystery; "maybe others get it but I don't."

And the power of the love of God is stifled—right there.

But wait! Before you glaze over and put this book down . . . there is a way through this.

Look at the verse from this perspective: It is your *separation* from God that was crucified with Christ, including all the sinful consequences of separation. That is what has died and has been destroyed forever. "Now all things are of God, who has reconciled us to Himself through Jesus Christ" (2 Cor. 5:18).

On the cross, Jesus crucified everyone and everything that was not of God, including your "old Adam" nature. That was your separated, sinful nature—the one that causes so very many problems and pains.

Seeing the verse from this perspective helps to set us free from being preoccupied with our little "i" that was crucified with Christ. Instead, we can start to give thanks and praise to God for setting us free from the curse of separation, and for bringing us into a totally new realm of being.

That new realm of being is invisible at first, but the more you look into it, the more it becomes real and tangible in your experience.

THE NEW REALM OF BEING IS CHRIST HIMSELF

Please look at your inheritance in Christ! It is awesome, and it is available for you here and now. It is waiting to be acknowledged and quickened and manifested in you and through you. It will never be forced upon you, because love never exerts force. Force is a power that the world uses, but the power of love is the opposite of force.

The power of love is humble, longsuffering, kind, and patient. Love beckons us, looks out for us, and never stops waiting for us. We should never doubt the invitation, and never fear that we have missed it. It is always there, waiting for us.

But the invitation is about relationship, and for any relationship to grow—and not remain stagnant—it needs to be nurtured. The way to develop relationship with the Author of love is to come to know Him through His Word. Jesus beckons us to Himself, urging us on—ever deeper into love: "Abide in Me, and I in you" (John 15:4).

Jesus could not have given us a more intimate invitation, could He?

I think many of us would like to accept His invitation to step into the Holy of Holies (that is, into union with God Himself) but find ourselves trapped in physicality. We find it hard to let go of the temporary physical form of the Son of Man and to identify with the eternal spiritual substance of the Son of God.

Perhaps this metaphor would help: The Lord spoke to the prophet Jeremiah about a potter who made a new vessel out of the clay of the original vessel, which had become spoiled: "And the vessel that he [the potter] made of clay was marred in the hand of the potter; so he made it again into another vessel, as it seemed good to the potter to make" (Jer. 18:4).

The Lord God is the potter, and the first vessel that He made was humankind. Humankind fell away from God and became most terribly marred. God could have destroyed that first vessel—or mold—and started again. But He did not. Instead, God chose to come down to earth as Jesus Christ, and He took upon Himself the covering of the marred mold. Another name for the mold is "old Adam"—and we were all included in "old Adam," as we saw in chapter 3.

On the cross, Jesus, "the last Adam" (1 Cor. 15:45), was crucified and the mold was obliterated and reduced to its original substance. Separation was obliterated, and yet the basic elements of that substance remained, ready to be reformed into the new creation. In the same way that a potter melts down the clay and uses the same substance to create a new vessel, so God "melted down" the particles of the old Adam, returning them to the quantum field.

God then purified and scoured clean the entire quantum field with the shed blood of Jesus, so that when God raised Jesus from the dead, He could create a completely new vessel that had no trace of sin, separation, or entropy. The new vessel is the new creation, created through Christ: "So if anyone is in Christ, there is a new creation: everything old has passed away; see, everything has become new!" (2 Cor. 5:17, NRSV).

The thing is, we appear to be human, and God gives us the freedom to choose to call ourselves human (that is, to identify with the old Adam). But that is the lie of Satan. The truth is that we are no longer mortal human beings and must not regard ourselves in this way, because "from now on, we regard no one according to the flesh" (2 Cor. 5:16).

Furthermore, the Word confirms that "as He [Jesus] is, so are we in this world" (1 John 4:17). After His resurrection, Jesus appeared to His disciples in a body, but it was no longer a limited human body. It was a spiritual body—Spirit made manifest in three-dimensional form—and it could penetrate walls, and travel through space, in an instant. It was no longer subject to decay and death. As was His body, so are our bodies, even now. For this our Savior died.

This time round, in contrast with His first creation, God ensured that this new creation would remain perfect forever, because Christ is immanent in every part of it: "He who descended is the very one who ascended higher than all the heavens, in order to fill the whole universe" (Eph. 4:10, NIV). Paul reiterates this truth in his letter to the church at Colossae: "there is neither Greek nor Jew, circumcised nor uncircumcised, barbarian, Scythian, slave nor free, but Christ is all and in all" (Col. 3:11).

Someone may ask, "If Christ fills all things, then why do we not see more Christlikeness? Why do we not see more expressions of love in the world?"

As we saw earlier, love never forces itself upon anyone, but looks for hearts that are open to receive and to believe. It is faith that quickens the things of Christ and brings them into manifestation. Faith is the "sixth sense" by which we perceive invisible spiritual truth and call it into visibility.

So let us waste no more time and let us move toward seeing. Let us come alongside Augustine of Hippo who said,

"Faith is to believe what we do not see, and the reward of that faith is to see what we believe."

So what is it that, at present, we do not see?

Our new life in Christ is spiritual and invisible. We do not "see" it, but it is more powerful than anyone or anything in the physical realm, and we see its effects. We do not "see" the Spirit, for example, but we see—progressively—the effects of the Spirit. We do not "see" love or hate. We do not "see" righteousness or sins. However, we certainly see the effects of all these qualities. That is how we know that they exist. In the same way, we know that the Spirit of Christ (the Holy Spirit) exists, because we can experience His effects in our lives and in the lives of others—if we are willing, and open to Him.

Therefore, let us not shy away from the things of the Spirit, for Spirit is the substance of our lives from here into eternity.

Look! "If the Son makes you free, you shall be free indeed" (John 8:36). But free from what? This short verse encompasses a multitude of glorious blessings:

By overturning the old order of things on the cross, the Son has set you free from sickness, disease, decay, and death. In fact, He has dealt with the root cause of this hellish quartet by abolishing entropy altogether.

Entropy is the gradual (or rapid) decline from order to disorder, and it was put into motion at the Fall, when humanity severed its lifeline with God. At that point, human beings began living as separated, closed systems which depended upon a limited, ever-reducing supply of life force. The apostle Paul calls it the law of sin and death.

In scientific terms, entropy is described in the second law of thermodynamics which states that within all things in the universe there is a relentless tendency towards chaos and disorder, and that left to themselves all things will eventually decay and die.

The only power strong enough to abolish entropy from the universe is the death and resurrection of Jesus Christ. When Christ reconciled all things to God, who is omnipresent Life, entropy lost its stranglehold on the universe: "For it pleased the Father . . . to reconcile all things to Himself, by Him, whether things on earth or things in heaven, having made peace through the blood of His cross" (Col. 1:19–20). It is entropy that leads to death and therefore, by definition, when Jesus set everyone free from death by "tast[ing] death for everyone" (Heb. 2:9), He also tasted entropy and abolished it completely. In its place, He ushered in the eternally life-giving Spirit and the fulness of life that He had planned to give us: "I have come that they may have life, and have it to the full" (John 10:10, NIV).

The Son has also set us free from space and time, which are linked to entropy and which are the cause of untold suffering. The limitations of space have been swept away by the omnipresent Spirit, as have the limitations of time and gravity.

The Son has indeed set us free from lack and limitation of all kinds. Where there is material, emotional, or intellectual lack, the Spirit of Christ provides abundant provision in the particular area of need: "God is able to make all grace abound toward you, that you, always having all sufficiency in all things, may have an abundance for every good work" (2 Cor. 9:8). Where there is limitation in the area of spiritual activity, Jesus freely bestows His authority: "Behold, I give you the authority to trample on serpents and scorpions, and over all the power of the enemy, and nothing shall by any means hurt you" (Luke 10:19).

The Father has given us all that we need to step into the glorious freedom of the children of God, through faith in His word.

How amazing it is to consider that we now have the same nature as our heavenly Father, because we have been born of Him. In the same way that we inherited our physical DNA and characteristics from our earthly parents, so—even more surely—have we inherited the DNA and the characteristics of God.

That means you have the "signature" of God pulsing in every one of the 30 trillion cells of your body. That is the life of Christ.

It is worth noting that every cell has roughly two trillion molecules, each performing with exquisite precision, and often within thousandths of a second—a biochemical dance. During a given moment in the life of a cell, thousands of events are being precisely coordinated at the molecular level. The fine-tuning of our God is stunning—at every level.

Just as the DNA of our righteous Father is dancing within us, so the fruit of the Spirit is flowing in us and through us. We can always draw on an abundance of the fruit of the Spirit which is "love, joy, peace, longsuffering, kindness, goodness, faithfulness, gentleness, self-control. Against such there is no law" (Gal. 5:22–23). They are the most powerful qualities in the universe because they are inseparable from the law of the Spirit of Christ, which is infinitely more powerful than the law of sin and death.

No wonder, then, that Jesus placed such emphasis on the need to be "born again" (John 3:3–7). All that He obtained for us on the cross—that is, His very life—can only be accessed through His Spirit.

Through faith in the sacrifice of Jesus on our behalf, we are now an integral part of the body of the risen Christ and are a partaker of the divine nature. We are no longer the son or the daughter of our parents; each of us is now the child of God, born of God, begotten of the Spirit.

We must believe that the Christ is now our true identity—not because an author or a preacher tells us so, but because the Lord Himself tells us so. He tells us very clearly and emphatically in His Word: "I have been crucified with Christ; it is no longer I who live, but Christ lives in me" (Gal. 2:20); "you died, and your life is hidden with Christ in God" (Col. 3:3).

If we do not embrace the truth that we are now spiritual beings and part of the body of the risen Lord, we miss the full impact of the blessings which have been showered upon us by God, who has "blessed us with every spiritual blessing in the heavenly places in Christ" (Eph. 1:3), and we deny ourselves access to the very same power that raised Jesus from the dead.

Chapter 5

Releasing the Power of God in Prayer

"RELEASING" IS THE KEY WORD OF THIS chapter's title. The power of God is always flowing through Christ: "Christ is the power of God and the wisdom of God" (1 Cor. 1:24). Christ does not only *have* power, but He *is* the power of God—and He is the same yesterday, today, and forever.

However, Christ does not force Himself upon us. He waits for us to respond in relationship and in faith, and then He is free to flow through us. It is striking that the declaration that God "is able to do exceedingly abundantly above all that we ask or think" is immediately qualified by these words: "according to [in proportion to] the power that works in us" (Eph. 3:20). In other words, it is not a "given": There are degrees of power that we can experience—or not—depending upon our responses and our choices.

God asks us to cooperate with Him, to enable His power to work within us and through us. During His days on earth, Jesus made it very clear that He does not work in isolation. Not at all. His very purpose in coming to earth was to reconcile the human race to God, and to co-opt men, women, and children to work with Him in ushering in His glorious kingdom: "we are His workmanship, created in Christ Jesus for good works" (Eph. 2:10).

Jesus also said, "As the Father has sent Me, I also send you" (John 20:21). In response, He calls us to make a conscious choice. However, that choice *does* require focused persistence on our part. We need to strive to abide in our true identity in Christ, and to keep His word living and active within us. It involves hard work, but it is more than worth it! It is wondrous and humbling indeed to realize that the King of kings waits upon us to further His work upon the earth.

If we have actively made the choice to be "labourers together with God" (1 Cor. 3:9, KJV), our question now is how to pray and what to pray for? It is to our Master that we look for the answers.

Jesus gives clear priority to the kingdom of God. In His Sermon on the Mount, He urges His disciples to "seek first the kingdom of God" (Matt. 6:33), shortly after teaching them to pray "May your kingdom come, and your will be done on earth as it is in heaven" (Matt. 6:10, PHILLIPS).

The kingdom of God is within those who believe (Luke 17:21). Therefore, when we ask for the kingdom to come—as Jesus has instructed us to do—the act of asking helps us to focus our inner eyes and our imagination on the kingdom and the characteristics of the kingdom. All our praying is directed toward bringing into manifestation the things of the kingdom of God, which is the new creation.

In other words, the aim of our prayers is to bring about a change of circumstance(s) which will reflect the characteristics of the kingdom: righteousness and justice, goodness and mercy, eternal and abundant life, love and forgiveness, joy and peace, health and wholeness, sufficiency, completeness and perfection. In the kingdom, there is no sickness or disease, no accidents, no broken relationships, no conflict, no pain, no sorrow, no death.

The first three gospels clearly show that the main reason God became incarnate in Jesus was to establish the Father's kingdom on earth, and He assures us that it is the Father's good pleasure to give us the kingdom (Luke 12:32).

Indeed, the main purpose of Jesus' miracles was to point toward the kingdom and to demonstrate that there is no sickness nor death nor lack and limitation there—on the contrary, that it is replete with love, joy, wholeness, and peace. He was giving us windows into the kingdom of God, and urging us to make the kingdom and God's righteousness the focus and priority in our lives.

However, while on earth, Jesus limited Himself to preaching and demonstrating the kingdom within the setting of "this world," because He had not yet gone to the cross to crucify "this world" and the "first Adam"; nor had He yet released His life as omnipresent Spirit. Whereas, unbelievable as it may sound, we who inherit the blessings of Jesus' death and resurrection have a much broader authority than He did (that is, before His crucifixion) to heal the sick, raise the dead, and overcome the other works of the devil. Why? Because, before His crucifixion, Jesus identified Himself completely with finite human form and all its limitations.

But now we, in our identity as adopted children of God, fully partake of Christ's life, which is spiritual and omnipresent. The Spirit of Christ was released throughout the whole universe after Jesus had ascended and returned to the Father: "He who descended is the very one who ascended higher than all the heavens, in order to fill the whole universe" (Eph. 4:10, NIV).

Jesus knew that His ascended Spirit would impart divine life to every atom throughout the universe. That is why He was able to give this astounding assurance to His disciples just before His arrest and crucifixion: "Most assuredly, I say to you, he who believes in Me, the works that I do he will do also; and greater works than these he will do, because I go to My Father" (John 14:12). He does not specify what the "greater works" are, but logically they must be related to ushering in the kingdom of God—the new creation—because that is what Jesus came to establish through His sacrifice on the cross, and through His resurrection and ascension.

One of the last statements—and, the last command—issued by Jesus to His disciple John in the book of Revelation, is: "Behold, I am making all things new. . . . Write, for these words are faithful and true [they are accurate, incorruptible, and trustworthy]" (Rev. 21:5, AMP).

"Behold, I am making all things new" is, in itself, an astounding statement by Jesus Christ. The words that follow it are all the more striking, because they reflect the urgency of His message. It goes without saying that any and every statement made by Jesus is faithful and true, and yet the Christ places such supreme emphasis on these lines that He instructs His disciple John to put down in writing that His words are indeed "faithful and true."

Should we not, therefore, pay very close attention to this emphasis, and ask what it means for us?

Another vital element in this verse is that Jesus is categorically saying, "I am making all things new." Not "I *will* make," but *"I am making,"* in the present tense. Furthermore, He says, "all things." Not just a few things—but everyone, everything, every situation, everywhere.

The question is: Do we take Jesus at His word? If we do not, then we will not see His word bearing fruit. However, if we do—then "Everything is possible for the one who believes" (Mark 9:23, NIRV).

Before He ascended to the Father, Jesus said, "you shall receive power when the Holy Spirit has come upon you; and you shall be witnesses to Me . . . to the end of the earth" (Acts 1:8). To be a witness is to provide proof that all that Jesus said and did was true.

All this would be an impossibility, a daydream, if Jesus had not also said: "Behold, I give you the authority to trample on serpents and scorpions, and over all the power of the enemy" (Luke 10:19). We have the authority of God Himself to overcome evil and the effects of the Fall—to overcome "this world" with its entropy, decay, and death.

However, we do not stop there—simply dealing with the destruction of the negative—because the Lord calls us onward to "bear fruit, and that your fruit should remain, that whatever you ask the Father in My name He may give you" (John 15:16). For that to happen, we need to follow the example set by our Master in dying to self, identifying with Him at every stage of His death, resurrection, and ascension. Then, going forth in Christ, standing firmly upon Galatians 2:20, we can take authority over the quantum field and all its constituent molecules and, in the power of the Holy Spirit, declare the Word of God which makes "all things new."

PRAYER AND THE MIRACLES OF JESUS

Jesus performed many miracles—miracles of nature, of raising the dead, of healing, and of abundant supply. His manner of prayer in almost all these circumstances was to speak a word or give a command, and sometimes He healed through touch. He never beseeched His Father to do the miracles. Rather, He trusted His Father to work through Him, and rested upon the authority that the Father had given to Him:

"All authority has been given to Me in heaven and on earth" (Matt. 28:18).

It is worth noting here that neither did Jesus' disciples beseech the Father. Following in the footsteps of their Master, they, in turn, caused miracles to occur by taking authority in the name of Jesus. You and I are called to do the same.

What was happening in people's bodies when they received healing, through the intervention of Jesus and His disciples?

Let us consider, for example, the healing of the two blind men who called out to Jesus as He was leaving Jericho (Matt. 20:29–34). Jesus touched their eyes, and they received their sight. The power of God flowing through Jesus altered the composition of the damaged cells in the two men's eyes and restored them to correct order. In other words, Jesus exercised authority in and through portions of the quantum field, in order to manifest the healing.

WHAT DOES "EXERCISING AUTHORITY THROUGH THE QUANTUM FIELD" MEAN?

In chapter 1, we saw that the universe is one vast, interlocking system of energy waves which is called the quantum field. It is the fundamental substance of all matter—be it subatomic particles, cells, molecules, bones, tissue, or arteries. So when Jesus healed the blind eyes, He used His God-given authority to rearrange the disorder in the cells and tissues of the two blind men and restore their sight.

Another of Jesus' miracles was the healing of the centurion's servant, who was paralyzed (Matt. 8:5–13). As a Roman soldier, with soldiers under his own authority, the centurion understood very well the power of authority and of commands. He said to Jesus, "Lord, I am not worthy that You should come under my roof. But only speak a word, and my servant will be healed" (Matt. 8:8)—and indeed he was healed.

This miracle is especially significant because it demonstrates that the power of God to heal and transform is not limited by distance. The Word of God and commands issued in His name exercise power wherever they are directed, at whatever the distance. Since the quantum field is one substance within the atmosphere of Spirit, which is One, there is in fact no substantial distance. It simply appears so to our limited senses.

Whether Jesus was physically present with a person or situation or not, spiritual power streamed from Him and rearranged the molecules that had gone awry in the physical bodies and in the circumstances that He encountered. In the same way that a magnet draws iron filings to itself—irresistibly—so the molecules bowed the knee, so to speak, in the presence of Jesus and rearranged themselves into correct order.

Love, and the effects of love, are irresistible. The people rejoiced to see blind eyes opened, deaf ears unstopped, the dead raised, and peace restored to the minds of people who had been tormented by evil spirits.

However, Jesus stressed that it was the God the Father who was doing all this work through Him: "I can of Myself do nothing" (John 5:30). If that is true of Jesus, then how much truer must it be of us?

Jesus calls us to be coworkers with Him, to bear fruit and to do the works that He did. But we must, in turn, rely on the Spirit of Christ to perform these works through us. It is only as we appropriate our new life in Christ and abide in Him, that we will see the power of God manifesting through us.

Jesus has given us all the authority we need to work miracles. Therefore, let us take Him at His word . . . and then watch as His love and power are released in ways that we could never even imagine.

But how do we obey Him and do what He asks of us?

The answer is: by getting ourselves out of the way. We cannot do any of these things in our own strength or intelligence. However, Christ can and will do them in us and through us, to the degree that we acknowledge Him to be our Savior—our very life and our very power to affect change. It is then that His righteousness becomes ours, and we can pray with expectant faith. "The prayer of the righteous is powerful and effective" (James 5:16, NRSV).

Ultimate power is not a force. It is a Person. It is Christ Himself. The exercise of ultimate power, therefore, requires relationship. As we have seen in earlier chapters, the nature of our relationship with Christ is more intimate than any other relationship we can describe or imagine. It is a relationship of oneness, attained through our faith in the death and resurrection of Jesus.

The poet Alfred Tennyson expresses the intimacy in this way: "Closer is He than breathing, and nearer than hands and feet." Language restricts us at this point, because the word "closer" and the scriptural phrases "in Christ" and "with Christ" all imply duality, whereas there is in fact no duality. You are one with Christ. As a member of the body of Christ, wherever He goes, you go, and whatever happens to Him happens to you.

Christ is infinite. You, too, are infinite.

However, this does not mean that you disappear into some amorphous cloud called "Christ" and lose all distinctiveness. Not at all. The Christ manifests Himself in an infinity of forms, each one bearing the characteristics and qualities of Christ, but distinctive.

Our model is the Godhead Itself: God the Father, God the Son, and God the Holy Spirit—three in one and one in three. As an adopted son or an adopted daughter in Christ, you are now fully embraced within the Holy Family. You are now Christ made manifest as one of His infinite, beloved expressions. So there is multiplicity, but it is all enfolded within the omnipresent God.

This all sheds light on your identity as a temple of the Holy Spirit, and the kingdom of God being within you (Luke 17:21). This awesome truth speaks of your spiritual identity as an adopted son or daughter of God.

While we are praying and looking for the kingdom, we take authority over situations that are plainly not God's will. Jesus gives us His authority and calls us to abide in Him—in the same way that the branch lives because it is connected to the vine: "I am the vine, you are the branches" (John 15:5). Thus connected to the ever-flowing source of "divine sap," we can set aside any tendency to be anxious or fearful, and trust Him to do the work through us: "For God has not given us a spirit of fear, but of power and of love and of a sound mind" (2 Tim. 1:7).

Abiding in Him—having our lives hidden with Christ in God—gives profound insight into the meaning of "praying in the name of Jesus." It means, literally, to let go of one's own name and identity, leaving them at the foot of the cross, and stepping into the very identity of Jesus. Therefore, we believe that it is Christ who is praying through us and as us. That is what it really means to "pray in His name"—the power of God can flow through unhindered, imparting grace upon grace.

It is significant that on six separate occasions, Jesus promises to grant us anything we ask "in My name" (John 14:13–14; 15:7, 16; 16:23–24). This is a staggering promise. We should heed the guidance of our Lord and Master who chose and appointed us, and who is constantly encouraging us on to bear fruit in prayer and in our lives.

It is significant that the original Greek word translated "ask" also conveys the idea of requesting or demanding. This ties in with Jesus' instruction elsewhere in the Gospels for us to take authority in His name.

We cannot go wrong if we base our prayers and commands upon the Word of God. There is no better model than the command that God Himself spoke repeatedly in the first chapter of Genesis: "Let there be . . ." In the name of Jesus, we can pray, "Let the new creation come"; "May Your kingdom come, may Your will be done on earth as it is in heaven"; "Let there be righteousness, let there be fulness of life, and let there be holiness and perfection"; and so forth.

The quantum field is now saturated with the Spirit of Christ, who fills the universe (Eph. 4:10), and God calls us to be coworkers in bringing in the harvest. But what does that mean? It means cooperating with the Holy Spirit, to be willing channels of the power of God to impact the quantum field with love, and to bring into visibility the new creation.

A good place to start is with our own bodies. Jesus calls us to be His witnesses, and part of our witness to Him is through our bodies.

Since you are a spiritual being, and the Spirit is the dominant power, you can take authority over your physical body and command it to come into line with God's pattern. You really can.

You can command the molecules that constitute your body to release their grip on the old Adamic mold, reminding them that Jesus crushed that corrupted mold upon the cross. The old mold no longer has any substance nor legal right to exist, because the law of the Spirit of life in Christ Jesus has set you free from the old Adamic law, or pattern of things (Rom. 8:2).

You remind those same molecules that they are saturated with the blood (that is, the life) of Christ, and then command them to come into line with His holy life. Let them manifest wholeness, peace, and the abundant life of Christ. In His life there can linger no arthritis, no cancer, no auto-immune diseases, no depression, no viruses or bacteria—and so on. No. In your new life in Christ, the fruit of the Spirit predominates and rules your body.

From there you can radiate outward and pray for other people and circumstances that come to your attention. In each situation, remember that Jesus has given you full authority to issue commands (based on His Word) in His name, in order to channel God's grace to those on whose behalf you are interceding.

Intercession is offering up our born-again, spiritual self to God so that He may use us to form His new creation.

When we speak out the Word of God and intercede, our understanding of the operation (the oneness) of the quantum field strengthens our faith. The words of God, either spoken out loud or prayed in silence, focus our intentions and course through the quantum field like lightning, affecting the object(s) of our intentions. In addition, because of the principle of oneness, it is logical to believe that these same prayers and words also affect and bless people, creatures, areas, and circumstances that are unknown to us.

It does not matter that we do not see the full impact of our prayers. In fact, not seeing helps to keep us humble and persistent. What matters above all is to be faithful to God's instructions in His Word, to do what we can and then to trust wholly in the working of the Holy Spirit, who desires to manifest the things of Christ on earth infinitely more than we do.

Chapter 6

How Faith Connects Us with God's Power

"... and this is my prayer. That God ... will give you
spiritual wisdom and the insight to know more of him:
that you may receive that inner illumination of the spirit
which will make you realise ... *how tremendous is the
power available to us who believe in God."*

— Ephesians 1:18–19, PHILLIPS, emphasis added

OUR VERSE ABOVE IS SAYING THAT GOD'S power is there, but
that it is not available in a general way. It is available to those
who have faith.

Faith is like a bridge into God's world. It enables us
to turn our backs on pain, distress, sickness, broken relationships, confusion, and grief, and open our hearts to
receive the healing, transforming grace of God. We do not
deny that the pains and griefs are terribly real—for they
are indeed real; but faith knows that there is an infinitely

more powerful reality waiting to be acknowledged and appropriated.

The exercise of faith hinges upon the free will that humankind was given at the beginning of creation. Without God's gift of free will—that is, if love was the established norm—then we would all be automatons, loving on command—and that is not love. Human beings exercised free will, and we went our own way. "All we like sheep have gone astray" (Isa. 53:6). The disastrous results are plain to see in the world in which we live.

When Jesus came into our midst, to rescue us, He not only took upon Himself all our sins and the effects of sin and made us new, born-again beings in Christ. He also gave us a particular gift, without which we could not receive His salvation—the gift of His faith. Not just "faith," which would be amazing in itself—but *His* faith: "I live by the faith of the Son of God, who loved me, and gave himself for me" (Gal. 2:20b, KJV). That is indeed amazing. We have within us the same faith that dwelt within Jesus while He was being tempted by Satan; while He was doing all His miracles; and while He was arrested, tortured, and led to the cross.

This is a powerful truth. However, we have to exercise our free will and choose to live in the flow of Jesus' faith. It is not forced upon us, but let us respond with our whole heart to God's desire that we embrace His Son's gift of supernatural faith. Let us then step into the living waters of His

Spirit—and see spiritual reality swimming into view here and now, on earth.

This truth is expressed in a beautiful way by the prophet Ezekiel, as he describes the river that flows from the temple of God (the throne of God): "[E]verything will live wherever the river goes. . . . Along the bank of the river . . . will grow all kinds of trees. . . . Their leaves will not wither, and their fruit will not fail" (Ezek. 47:9, 12). The river is the Spirit of God. Wherever the Spirit of God is acknowledged and released through faith and in prayer, it brings life—abundant life on earth now, and into eternity.

Looking out upon this world with its terrors, violence, and pain beyond measure, it is easy to think, "What difference does it make if I pray, anyway?"

It makes an enormous, incalculable difference.

Even at the physical, material level, it is now well known that observation and *intention* make a distinct and observable impact on the quantum field, altering the formation of subatomic particles. Therefore, how much greater is the impact when we pray and issue Word-based commands, in faith, in the name of Jesus, before whom every knee must bow—not just human knees but every subatomic particle in existence.

The Word of God itself contains immeasurable power— it is always living and active for those who will put their trust in it. The psalmist declares that the Word of God is of such unutterable value that the Father esteems it even above His own holy name: "You have magnified Your word above all Your name" (Ps. 138:2). The significance of this is profound, at so many levels: God exalts His word for our benefit—to communicate to us His love, His nature, His salvation, and His purposes.

The Word of God is Spirit: "The words that I speak to you are spirit," said Jesus to His disciples (John 6:63). It is dominant over anything and everything in the physical and spiritual realms. It is the creative force, the parent force.

If the Word of God is dominant over everything, why do we so seldom see its effects on earth? Because the muscle of faith is required in order to bring the spiritual truth(s) inherent in the Word into manifestation. In chapter 4 of Hebrews we read that the Israelites missed out on the supreme blessing that God had planned for them—to bring them into the Promised Land—because they had heard the Word of God on the matter but did not believe it: "the word which they heard did not profit them, not being mixed with faith in those who heard it" (Heb. 4:2).

It seems shocking that even Jesus could not overrule the barrier of unbelief, but that is because the requirement for faith is a spiritual principle laid down by God Himself. On a visit to His hometown, Nazareth, we are told: "He could do no mighty work there, except that He laid His hands on a few sick people and healed them. And He marvelled because of their unbelief" (Mark 6:5–6).

Although shocking, this incident also conveys a gloriously positive message—that is, that the desire and intention of God is to manifest goodness and healing. If the world does not see it, it is *not* because God is withholding His transforming power. On the contrary, it is always available and waiting to be released through people of faith. Jesus Christ Himself says: "Most assuredly, I say to you, he who believes in Me, the works that I do he will do also; and greater works than these he will do, because I go to My Father" (John 14:12).

The terrible momentum of accumulated sin and evil in the world tends to blind us to the truth that in Christ we have all the power we need to be channels of transformation and renewal. The only way we can do that, though, is to cleave to Him and to meditate upon the Word of God, so that it becomes an integral part of our mind and starts to manifest in and through our lives. What we think about, during the day and the night, is extremely important.

Psychologists generally agree that our lives go in the direction of our most dominant thoughts, and that believers and nonbelievers alike can affect their lives positively or negatively by their patterns of thinking. How much truer this is of those people who choose to line their thoughts up with those of the Maker of the universe.

Practice is required, though, because we are swimming against the tide of the world; it takes effort and concentration if we are to avoid being trapped in "old Adam" patterns.

Paul knew all about that tendency and gives this exhortation in his letter to the Romans: "Don't let the world around you squeeze you into its own mould, but let God re-mould your minds from within" (Rom. 12:2, PHILLIPS). And he gives an equally inspiring call to the Philippians: "Let this mind be in you which was also in Christ Jesus" (Phil. 2:5).

In addition to personal effort and concentration, it is even more important to trust the Holy Spirit to guide you and lead you, otherwise it can become a mechanical process of the intellect. It is the Holy Spirit who "will guide you into all truth" (John 16:13) and apply the reality of the death and resurrection in Christ to each personal life. We cannot do that of our own will—it comes purely by grace and faith: "you were also raised with him through faith in the power of God, who raised him from the dead" (Col. 2:12, NRSV).

As we abide in the Word of God and trust Him to do the remolding, we find that, progressively, our old Adamic mind is actively being transformed into the mind of Christ.

The mind of Christ is a person—the Lord Himself. It is also a state of faith, which can be described as a state of awareness or consciousness. When the Lord Jesus walked this earth, He was *aware* of goodness—of love, fulfilment, and wholeness, despite being surrounded by hostility, lack, and disease—and He demonstrated that same awareness through His many miracles. This is because Jesus' inner gaze was constantly fixed upon His Father: "The Son can do nothing of Himself, but what He sees the Father do;

for whatever He does, the Son also does in like manner" (John 5:19).

What the Father does is always loving, life-giving, and gloriously transforming. Likewise, the mind of Jesus Christ was—and is—saturated with the glorious truths of the kingdom of God. The grace of God flowed out from Him, and miracles of transformation sprang up all around Him. In other words, the faith or state of awareness (consciousness) of Jesus created the reality He was already seeing with His inner eyes. It is for this reason that He says, "Do not judge according to appearance, but judge with righteous judgement" (John 7:24) and, "You judge according to the flesh; I judge no one" (John 8:15).

As you abide more and more in Christ—in the truth of who you are in Christ—you will find that your very thoughts and desires actually act as prayers and commands. They do not always need to be articulated. You are in an attitude, or consciousness, of prayer and thus fulfilling the command in 1 Thessalonians 5:17 to "pray without ceasing." The more attuned you become to God and His Word, the more His power flows out through you to bless others, without you even being aware that you are making a difference. In that state, you can say that your consciousness (or state of faith) is drawing forth the truth of God.

Flawed consciousness creates flawed reality—as we see all around us. However, consciousness of who we are in Christ creates godly reality. In effect, Jesus is saying to us,

"Come on, you can do this too! You can look behind the sick, hostile, decaying appearance, and see what the Father already sees—wholeness and beauty. And the more you keep your gaze upon the things of the kingdom, as revealed in the Word of God, the more you will see those things materialize before your very eyes."

The apostle Paul had tremendous insight into this; that is why he urges us to "seek those things which are above, where Christ is" (Col. 3:1) and to "Set your mind on things above" (Col. 3:2)—not to escape from the trials of the world (as some have suggested), but in fact to impact the world for good in a much greater measure.

But we need to practice, practice, practice.

The mind is like a little piglet's curly tail. However much you may gently straighten out the tail and hold it straight, the moment you let go, it quickly coils back into its original curl. Likewise, the mind goes straight back to its old, familiar patterns of thinking. But the Holy Spirit is there to help us and strengthen us. As we keep returning to truth, continually bringing our attention back to the Word of God—practicing, practicing and never giving up, no matter how many times our minds recoil in piglet-tail fashion—we will see a difference. And that will greatly encourage us to press on.

Chapter 7

Meditation and Prayer—Some Practical Steps

MEDITATION

WHEN JESUS SAID, "IF YOU ABIDE IN ME, and My words abide in you" (John 15:7), He was pointing us toward meditation. The word "meditation" simply means focusing and pondering on something, to let it saturate your mind. Unlike New Age meditation, which usually advocates emptying the mind, Christian meditation calls us to do the opposite—to fill our minds with God and His truth. Jesus asks us to let Him and His word remain alive and active in our minds and hearts.

The Old Testament men and women of God were well acquainted with the power of meditating on the Word of God—and this despite the fact that they did not have the permanently indwelling Spirit to empower their meditations, as we do now. One example is when the Lord declared the vital importance of meditation to Joshua, when he was appointed to lead the children of Israel after Moses' death. The Lord said: "This Book of the Law [that is, the Word of God] shall not depart from your mouth, but you shall meditate in it day and night . . . and then you will have good success" (Josh. 1:8).

The "good success" that is the result of abiding in the Word includes the process of "the renewing of your mind" (Rom. 12:2). For that is the aim of meditation: that our former, worldly ways of thinking be replaced, progressively, by the thoughts and attitudes of Christ. As our minds are renewed in this way, we come increasingly into alignment with God's will for our minds and our lives, and in accord with the command, "Let the same mind be in you that was in Christ Jesus" (Phil. 2:5, NRSV).

The more we are in line with the thoughts and desires of Christ, the more freedom the Holy Spirit has to pour out the "tremendous power" of Ephesians 1:19 through our prayers and words—when there is no resistance from our little "self." A rather crude but vivid analogy is to see ourselves as pipes designed to channel water from a faucet. A pipe can easily become encrusted with limescale. In that condition, water can still trickle through to a limited degree, but the flow is weak and intermittent. However, if the limescale (our wrong thinking) is dissolved through regular, faith-inspired meditation upon the Word of God, water (the Holy Spirit) can flow through unimpeded—and in power.

In this way, we come into right alignment with Christ and we walk, more and more, in His righteousness. Then we can begin to prove that "The prayer of a righteous person is powerful and effective" (James 5:16, NIV). We can never be righteous in our own strength, but faith-filled meditation enables us to "enter into" the righteousness of Jesus, and to walk in all that He has gained for us.

The importance of meditation, of keeping our minds stayed on Christ and His Word, receives considerable emphasis in the New Testament. Paul urges believers to "Let the word of Christ dwell in you richly" (Col. 3:16)—to fix your eyes on Jesus, to fix your minds on things above. He also says to Timothy, "Meditate on these things; give yourself entirely to them" (1 Tim. 4:15) ("these things" being the things of God, including His Word).

Meditation is a powerful tool provided by the Holy Spirit to explore the things of God in depth, and to enable us to bring the Word of God to life in our experience. The Word of God is Spirit—it is the Spirit of Jesus Christ Himself. Therefore, when we meditate in faith, we are inviting the Spirit right into our brains and bodies, where the Spirit progressively brings them into line with God's grace-filled pattern.

Depending upon your situation, you may choose to seek out and meditate upon scriptures that relate to the love of God, His forgiveness, His righteousness, His omnipotence,

His salvation, faith, and so on. The Holy Spirit will lead you if you seek His guidance.

In particular, I would encourage you to set aside time to study and meditate upon scriptures that speak of who you are in Christ. Those are the scriptures that will enable you to step into your new spiritual identity, and to start to experience the power of God as it flows in you and through you. Some key verses are 2 Corinthians 5:14–21; Galatians 2:20 and 6:14; Ephesians 2:5–6; and Colossians 3:3.

Do not look for particular "experiences," or place too much importance on feelings, which can be misleading. The key is to persist in faith and to place a priority on knowing who you are in Christ. If you don't know who you are, nor actively believe who you are, you will not be able to release what you have.

The process of dropping one's own identity and "putting on" Christ's identity requires daily practice; it cannot be attained overnight. The "default" program in every human being is "me" and "mine." It takes ongoing discipline to step down from the saddle and hand the reins over to Jesus, hour by hour, day by day. This is why even someone with the spiritual stature and experience of the apostle Paul declared, "I die daily" (1 Cor. 15:31). How much more, therefore, do *we* need to "die daily" to self and to reckon ourselves dead— yet alive in our new being in Christ?

It is indeed a lifelong process. However, we are much encouraged along the way as we see the fruits of meditating and praying in this way in our own lives and the lives of those for whom we pray.

Meditation does not necessarily require us to sit in the silence with our eyes closed. That is a good position, but sometimes our minds can wander or we nod off. The important thing is not to give up or feel disheartened—simply gently bring your mind back to the verse(s) or truths you are focusing upon. Pondering over the verses out loud is helpful, and I personally find that walking in a quiet environment while meditating and praying out loud is one of the best ways to keep the mind focused and to enable the Holy Spirit to flow more freely. Try to recall your scriptures at regular intervals while you are at work, going about your daily tasks, and so on.

During any initiative to deepen your prayer life—and in particular, any move to align yourself with your identity in Christ—the human mind is likely to rebel and to want to throw in the towel on many occasions. That is absolutely normal. However, if that *does* happen, please resist the temptation to give up, and do not be fooled by the enemy into thinking that you are a failure and that you can never progress.

Looking back on my initial years of trying to deepen my spiritual life, I see now that I spent far too long stuck in the deadening mire of "repentance mode," looking at my own failures in prayer instead of looking up and outward to the one source of true life. There is, of course, a place for genuine repentance for sin, but with hindsight I can see that basically I was trying to repent of not being able to live the Christian life. That was nothing else but my pride. Of *course* I could not live the Christian life! Only one person can live it, and that is Christ Himself. It eventually began to dawn on me that pride does not necessarily take the form of arrogance, which is easy to spot. A less obvious form of pride is an ongoing feeling of inadequacy and failure. But that is still pride, because the underlying concept is that believers can muster up some goodness in their own strength, rather than relying totally upon Christ. The situation changed markedly when I began to base my spiritual life on the truth of God's Word, in a much more focused way, instead of mixing it with my own changeable feelings and perceptions.

At the start, a verse you take into meditation may feel like a dry mental concept, and it will seem foolish to the human mind. However, with persistence, it begins to drip-drip throughout your being—in the same way that a small drop of ink spreads through a glass of water, gently infusing it with color—and eventually you find that the Holy Spirit begins to quicken to you the deeper meaning of the verse.

Then comes your exclamation: "Oh, I see!" The eureka moment. I was once blind but now I see. As when a flash of lightning illuminates the whole landscape, where once all you could see were steep, dark, and impenetrable mountains, now verdant valleys, beautiful mountain passes, and meandering rivers suddenly come into view. In other words, meditation opens up for you a reality that you never knew existed.

However, the "seeing" has to be a spiritual seeing, for the things of God are foolishness to the natural mind. Never be discouraged. God wants us to grasp His life and His truth infinitely more than we want to—so press in and rely on His Holy Spirit to help you and to guide you into all truth.

Again, it is strengthening to remember that Jesus Christ Himself is the Word of God (Rev. 19:13). Therefore, when we meditate on scriptures we are engaging with Jesus Christ at a very profound level.

PRAYER

We have seen in chapters 3 and 4 the power of shedding our own identity, stepping into Christ, and praying "in the name of Jesus." We do not use the name of Jesus as a mantra, but rather, increasingly cause it to become alive in us through faith, pondering, meditation, and prayer.

From there, we can give thanks to Jesus for the authority He has given us to overcome all the works of the enemy, and that nothing shall by any means hurt us (Luke 10:10), so we can take authority in His name with confidence.

The power that God makes available to us is indeed awesome. Not only do we have the privilege of praying in the name of omnipotence, but we also have the right to wield the sword of the Spirit—the Word of God—into any situation. The creative power of a command issued in accord with Scripture is far greater than we can think or imagine.

REMEMBER YOUR TRUE IDENTITY

As often as you can, and especially when you are about to pray and intercede, it is important to remind yourself of the identity that we inherited in Christ as soon as we placed our trust in Him. Do not go by feelings, nor by what your senses tell you, but make a firm decision to believe the Word of God. I would encourage you to draw up a list of scriptures that tell you who you are in Christ, and to keep them alive in your mind as much as possible.

The following is a short example of how to recall our identity in Christ, which I am expressing here as a prayer to God. There are many other relevant scriptures affirming the same truths, upon which you can draw and make the prayer your own. If the pronoun "I" is changed to "we," this prayer can also become a powerful form of intercession:

> Righteous Father, I give You thanks and praise that You have chosen me in Christ Jesus since before the foundation of the world (Eph. 1:4), and that these facts are now true about my new identity: When Jesus died on the cross I died with Him (Gal. 2:20), and I was also raised with Him (Col. 2:12), and my life is now hidden with Christ in God (Col. 3:3). I am now born again—born of

God and one with Him in Spirit (1 Cor. 6:17). I have been given the mind of Christ (1 Cor. 2:16), I am complete in Him (Col. 2:10), and I am a partaker of the divine nature (2 Pet. 1:4).

My body is now the temple of the Holy Spirit and I am not my own; I was bought at a price (1 Cor. 6:19–20). "I work hard with all the strength of Christ. His strength works powerfully in me" (Col. 1:29, NIRV). I have been chosen by Jesus and appointed to go and bear fruit, fruit that will remain (John 15:16). To that end, Christ has instructed me to pray in His name, and He has given me authority over all the power of the enemy, and nothing shall by any means hurt me (Luke 10:19). Christ has also assured me that, because I believe in Him, I will do the same works that He does, and even greater works (John 14:12). Amen.

PRAYING FOR HEALING

Once we have taken time to "climb up" into our true identity in Christ, through thanksgiving, meditation and prayer, we can go forward in faith to intercede. Our prayers of intercession can cover multiple needs; however, a large percentage of requests or needs for prayer often concern healing in some form.

Let us therefore take, as our example, someone who asks for prayer because he or she is suffering from cancer. I'll use the name "Jane." For the word "cancer" we can substitute any number of needs—be they physical, mental, emotional, spiritual, or circumstantial. The principle of prayer is the same for all of them.

The words will vary of course, and there are many different scriptures upon which to stand, but here is a sample meditation that comes as I sit in prayer now:

> Our Righteous Father, Lord Jesus Christ our Savior, Holy Spirit of God, our indwelling Lord, we praise You for Your boundless love and Your forgiveness. We praise You for coming to planet earth in the form of a human being to die for us, to pay the debt that we owe, and to make us partakers of the very life of God.
>
> We thank You for Jane, and that You chose her in Christ even before the creation of the world. You foresaw all her needs, her sicknesses, and sorrows, and You provided for them all—to set her free to live the life in all its fullness that You came to give her (John 10:10).
>
> I praise You that when You went to the cross, You not only took Jane there with You, but You also took upon Yourself all her sins and all her diseases and pains: "Surely he took up our pain and bore our suffering. . . . [H]e was pierced for

our transgressions, he was crushed for our iniqui-
ties; the punishment that brought us peace was
on him, and by his wounds we are healed" (Isa.
53:4–5, NIV).

The enemy will do all he can to persuade us that You
have not done all this for Jane. But he is a liar. It is
Your Word we choose to believe, not Satan's lies.

You call us instead to open our eyes and to see
all that You have done for us, and continue to do
for us. Your Word declares that "in Him we live
and move and have our being" (Acts 17:28). As
an adopted child of Yours, born of the Spirit, Jane
now has a secure dwelling place in the kingdom,
protected from the works of the evil one. You
have "delivered us from the power of darkness
and conveyed us into the kingdom of the Son of
His love" (Col. 1:13).

Furthermore, Jesus says that "the kingdom of
God is within you" (Luke 17:21) and urges us
to "seek first the kingdom and His righteousness,
and all these things shall be added to you" (Matt.
6:33). All that we need is already contained in the
kingdom of God within us, through Your Spirit.

Standing upon these truths, we bring all our problems to You, Father, and we ask to see the reality

of the kingdom in exchange. We bring Jane to You and ask to see Your kingdom made manifest right where this cancer appears to be, and where fear and doubt appear to press upon her. We ask for Your perfect will for Jane to be unveiled, right where she is now.

We take up the authority given to us by Jesus and we command all the molecules constituting Jane to release and let go of the old Adamic mold that is harboring cancerous cells. We know that in Christ there is no such thing as a cancerous cell, and we envisage every one of those cells as being saturated with the blood (that is, the life) of Christ Jesus.

We declare that the cancer that belonged to Jane's old-Adam body has now been obliterated on the cross with Jesus. Her current body is inseparable from Christ, and is a completely new creation. Therefore, cancer and pain no longer belong to her. They have lost their legal right to remain in the temple of the Holy Spirit, which Jane now is.

In the name of Jesus, we proclaim that "if anyone is in Christ, there is a new creation: everything old has passed away; see, everything has become new!" (2 Cor. 5:17, NRSV). Therefore, we stand upon this word and command that all the errant cells in Jane bow the knee to the Word of God and come into alignment with the truth—with Your wholeness and perfection.

Indeed, we send forth this same command to every single molecule in her body, that it align itself with the Christ and bring forth the new creation—the Kingdom of God—that Christ came to usher in: "Behold, I make all things new" (Rev. 21:5).

Father, we praise You that it is never Your will that any of Your children suffer. It is Your will that we understand all that You have done for us, and Your will that we believe You and walk in the overcoming life that You came to give us.

We therefore stand in faith upon the "blank check" promises in John's gospel, asking in the name of Jesus that You would empower our commands and prayers for Your glory, and that You would forgive us if we have prayed amiss in any way.

May Your Kingdom come and may Your will be done, on earth as it is in heaven. We give You thanks and praise and worship. Amen.

THE IMPORTANCE OF PERSEVERANCE AND PATIENCE

In essence, then, to pray as Jesus taught us is first to acquire the right to use His name; and then, using His name, to pray and command in line with the Word of God—above all, to pray for the kingdom to come. If we do this, we will be following strictly in the way shown to us by the Master.

However, we must not be looking out from the corner of our eyes to see whether our prayers are bearing fruit. Bearing fruit is the responsibility of the Holy Spirit, whereas our responsibility is simply to believe and to go on believing and praying.

It is very likely that, in order to develop our faith and strengthen our spiritual muscles, the Holy Spirit may keep us waiting. The Red Sea did not part until the chariots were virtually upon the Hebrews. The Jordan did not dry up until the Hebrews had first gotten their feet wet. The walls of Jericho did not fall until the last blast. Jesus did not hold out His hand to Peter until the latter was sinking.

In order to encourage us to pray faithfully and persistently, Jesus gave us the parable of the insistent widow who would not give up asking until the judge answered her request. He also told of the man who did not stop knocking until his neighbor got up to give him bread. These parables speak of bold and patient faith. Waiting on God and abiding in His Word in this way keeps us humble, heightens the sense of our need for Him, and causes us to experience His presence in deeper ways.

Therefore, using His name, we keep praying and asking for the kingdom to come, and we wait in expectation and thanksgiving.

The most important thing is to stay centered on Christ and to remember that "He who is in you is greater than he who is in the world" (1 John 4:4). Believe that He is directing the earthly molecular traffic within you and around you, for He not only moves mountains but the molecules and atoms that constitute them as well. We don't need to grit our teeth either, for God is infinitely more desirous to demonstrate wholeness through our prayers than we are to see it. We can put all our weight on these tender and reassuring words of Jesus: "Do not be afraid, little flock, for your Father has been pleased to give you the kingdom" (Luke 12:32, NIV).

Chapter 8

The Power of Oneness in Christ, and Its Implications for Believers

A drop of water that merges with the Atlantic Ocean
acquires the power of all seven oceans.

THIS SAYING IS A PROFOUND METAPHOR FOR WHAT Jesus
Christ has accomplished through His death and resurrection. By dissolving separateness, He drew each little droplet
of the human race into Himself, granting each droplet the
supreme gift of omnipresence.

Up until now, Christian theologians have tended to
resist this process of merging with the Infinite. Some have
dismissed it as "oriental religion" or "New Age philosophy."
This is a gross misinterpretation, and it dismisses the discoveries of modern physics that point towards an infinite
universe. Above all, it ignores verses in the New Testament
which explicitly state that God is omnipresent: "There is one
body and one Spirit . . . one God and Father of all, who is
above all, and through all, and in all" (Eph. 4:4, 6). Earlier

in the book of Ephesians, Christ is described as "the one who fills the whole wide universe" (Eph. 1:23, PHILLIPS). To the Colossian church Paul writes: "Christ is all and in all" (Col. 3:11).

It may help to look briefly at how New Testament and New Age philosophies each view the omnipresent or universal Christ. The three scriptures quoted above are true for everyone. However, they can only be brought into a person's experience through faith in the death and resurrection of Jesus Christ.

There is the nub: There lies a vast difference between New Testament truth and New Age philosophies. The latter states that God is all there is, and that therefore all human beings are inherently divine. They maintain that, in order to live peacefully and harmoniously, human beings need to "realize" their inner divinity—which is also referred to as the real self, higher consciousness, or even Christ-consciousness.

However, the truth is that by sidestepping Jesus' work on the cross, separation and dualism remain firmly entrenched in human consciousness. No amount of meditating or declaring that we are all divine will overcome the chasm of separation that can only be bridged by the redemption of Jesus.

So we can see that New Testament believers and New Age philosophies arrive at the same conclusion . . . but for *completely* different reasons. It is important to bring light to bear on both of them, cast out the lies, and then know and rest peacefully in the truth: "you shall know the truth, and the truth shall make you free" (John 8:32).

Above all, it is vital that we hold fast to the truth that the very reason that Jesus came to earth was to redeem us and to bring us back into union with the Godhead—in other words, into the very heart of the universal Christ. There is no more separation.

The reluctance of theologians to fully embrace the implications of quantum physics (that describe the nature and behavior of matter and energy at subatomic levels) brings to mind the obstacles faced by Galileo Galilei some four hundred years ago, when he dared to suggest that the earth was not the center of the universe and that it revolved around the sun. At the time, the church pronounced his proposition to be "false and contrary to Scripture."

The discoveries of quantum physics are as momentous as Galileo's discovery—in fact, much more so for Christians, because of their implications for the comprehension of the Christian faith and its practice. They certainly cannot be pronounced contrary to Scripture and, like Galileo's discovery, they will gather much greater momentum and significance as time goes on.

Western culture, in particular, has been progressively steeped in individualism, especially since the seventeenth century with the introduction of the Age of Rationalism (also known as the Enlightenment). In particular, the discoveries and thinking of Isaac Newton and René Descartes set the scene for the Cartesian-Newtonian paradigm, which assumed that the world consists of separate bits of matter. Furthermore, the paradigm assumed that matter and mind were two finite substances. In other words, dualism could not have been set in more solid concrete.

It was Einstein, a little more than one hundred years ago, who started the process of dismantling the dualistic edifice with his discovery that matter and energy are in fact the same, and that matter is simply frozen energy.

It is worth noting how, over the centuries, physicists who had proudly placed matter on a pedestal progressively destroyed their own foundations. First, they reduced hard chunky matter to invisible and intangible particles and called them molecules. Then they disaggregated the molecules to atoms, and progressively reduced atoms to quarks and mesons and gluons—the latter being the "glue" that held the former together—all of them invisible and intangible. Progressively, these pieces lost even their claim to be particles, and became waves upon an infinite ocean.

Without faith, human beings have fragmented this infinite ocean into finite quarks, mesons, gluons, and so forth—because the finite cannot comprehend the infinite. However, those who believe in the omnipresence of Christ's Spirit gain insight into the truth that the whole of reality is, in fact, an infinite ocean of Spirit: "He who descended is the very one who ascended higher than all the heavens, in order to fill the whole universe" (Eph. 4:10). Whoever, through faith in God's Word, can break out of the boundaries of individuality merges with the ocean of Spirit, which is responsive to thought, consciousness, and prayer. However, this "merging" does not mean the shrinkage or loss of a person's individual identity. On the contrary: It heralds his or her expansion to infinity.

As we saw earlier in this chapter, Christ Himself is the infinite ocean of Spirit because He "is all and in all" (Col. 3:11). Whoever believes in and identifies with Christ is absorbed into Him, and whatever happened to Him happened to us. When He died we died with Him, and when He was resurrected we were resurrected with Him.

It is helpful to note that although the discoveries by physicists and cosmologists do not in themselves prove scriptural truth, they certainly support it. Above all, they enable us to comprehend or gain deeper insight into passages of the Bible that previously seemed beyond the grasp of the intellect.

Take, for example, Paul's declaration in 2 Corinthians 5:14 that "if One died for all, then all died." In response, we may ask: How can it be that all of us—that is, untold billions of us—died when Jesus died? Some may say that it is simply a metaphor, but scientific insights enable us to go beyond metaphor to see how it was indeed possible for all humankind to have died when Jesus Christ died.

It helps to step back and see the overall picture from the beginning of time. Let's review our placement in Christ from the very start, and trace our ongoing position in Him right through to the resurrection and the ascension.

It is God the Father who placed us in His Son: "of Him [God] you are in Christ Jesus" (1 Cor. 1:30)—the very Son through whom the Father created the universe and everything in it. Several scriptures testify to the fact that everything was made in and through Jesus Christ: "For in him all things were created: things in heaven and on earth, visible and invisible. . . . He is before all things, and in him all things hold together" (Col. 1:16–17, NIV). In John's gospel, Jesus Christ is referred to as the Word through whom all things came into existence: "In the beginning was the Word. . . . All things were made through Him" (John 1:1, 3).

Jesus Christ was the singular point at the time of creation. This is the first step in the Father's movement toward self-expression in a three-dimensional form. It was from here that the quantum field emerged, providing the substance of three-dimensional creation. All the elements that were to constitute the entire human race, and everything else, were contained in the Christ. Many, if not most, cosmologists now agree that the universe was created at a singular moment called the Big Bang. All that can be observed in the universe—the 100 billion galaxies and everything we see around us on our own planet earth—began as a miniscule point that was small enough to fit through the eye of a needle. The universe emerged and rapidly spread out from that point. From the moment of creation and the expansion that followed, all that was to be required for human life (and everything else in the universe) was created.

It is an astounding fact that all the subatomic particles and elements that now constitute you and me were already in existence from the creation of the world. To put it another way: The subatomic particles that now constitute you were already contained in Christ at the point of creation.

When Christ became incarnate on earth as Jesus of Nazareth, He was fully man and fully God. Therefore, in His Godhead, He still contained all that the Father had placed within Him at the beginning of creation. That is why, when He hung on the cross and died, He was able to take all of humanity and the world down to the tomb with Him: "if One died for all, then all died" (2 Cor. 5:14); "God forbid that I should boast except in the cross of our Lord Jesus Christ, by whom the world has been crucified to me, and I to the world" (Gal. 6:14).

Because we had been placed in Christ by the Father, wherever Jesus Christ went we were with Him. When He went to the cross, we went with Him and died with Him there.

Knowing our position in Christ also sheds invaluable light on the fact that when Jesus was raised from the dead, we were raised together with Him and in Him. That is the whole purpose of the Incarnation: "God . . . made us alive together with Christ . . . and raised us up together . . . in Christ Jesus" (Eph. 2:4–6).

THE LORD'S SUPPER

The Lord's Supper is the ultimate expression of the Incarnation, and of our oneness with Christ. I hesitate to write about this holy mystery, because no human words could ever convey the infinite depths of its significance. On the other hand, I feel it would be wrong to omit it completely. Therefore, I would like to offer—very tentatively, indeed—a few short reflections within the context of this book.

The Lord's Supper is the term used in the New Testament (1 Cor. 11:20) to describe the Passover meal that Jesus shared with His disciples shortly before His arrest and crucifixion. It is also known as Holy Communion, Eucharist, Mass, and Blessed Sacrament, among other terms.

The fullest description of the meal is given by the apostle Paul, who passed on to the Corinthian church the following instructions, which he had received directly from Jesus Christ: "For I received from the Lord that which I also delivered to you: that the Lord Jesus on the same night in which He was betrayed took bread; and when He had given thanks, He broke it and said, 'Take, eat; this is My body which is broken for you; do this in remembrance of Me.' In the same manner He also took the cup after supper, saying, 'This cup is the new covenant in My blood. This do, as often as you drink it, in remembrance of Me.' For as often as you eat this bread and drink the cup, you proclaim the Lord's death until He comes" (1 Cor. 11:23–26).

The purpose of the Lord's Supper, as we can see, is infinitely rich. If taken regularly, it is an ongoing and tangible reminder of God's love and of Jesus' sacrifice on the cross to set us free from our sin.

It also conveys the spiritual truth that the old form of relationship between God and humankind—in which God was "out there," and human beings were separated and trapped in the "old Adam" nature—was broken wide open, just as Jesus' own body was broken, for that very purpose.

In other words, the old order of sin and death was, at that moment of sacrifice, replaced by the new order (the new covenant). The veil of separation was torn apart, and the Spirit of Christ was released by the Father to course through the universe, announcing freedom for every single person who will receive it: "For the law of the Spirit of life in Christ Jesus has set you free from the law of sin and death" (Rom. 8:2).

In addition to helping us remember Jesus' sacrifice and teaching us the spiritual meaning of what He accomplished for us on the cross, the Lord's Supper is also a vital means of strengthening our faith that Christ lives in us—that He becomes incarnate in us, and that we are one body in Him. The apostle Paul wrote, "The cup of blessing which we bless, is it not a very sharing in the blood of Christ? When we break the bread do we not actually share in the body of Christ? The very fact that we all share one bread makes us all one body" (1 Cor. 10:16–17, PHILLIPS).

This echoes the words of Jesus from earlier in His ministry, when He was teaching in the synagogue in Capernaum. It was then that He dropped the bombshell that caused many of His followers to abandon Him: "unless you eat the flesh of the Son of Man and drink His blood, you have no life in yourselves. . . . He who eats My flesh and drinks My blood abides in Me, and I in him" (John 6:53, 56).

These are extremely strong words, and it is understandable that many who heard them could not cope with what sounded like cannibalism. However, Jesus then proceeded to say something which seemingly contradicted His statement about the importance of consuming "flesh and blood": "It is the Spirit who gives life; the flesh profits nothing; the words that I speak to you are spirit and are life" (John 6:63).

So what did Jesus mean? Clearly, He did not mean that He was offering His literal flesh and His literal blood, there and then, for human beings to eat and drink. Was He then speaking entirely at the level of metaphor?

May I suggest that in light of what we have been exploring in this book—that is, the omnipresence of Christ throughout the entire substance of the universe—that it is indeed possible to consume Christ in a literal way? Allow me to explain further.

If we believe that the Spirit of Christ is omnipresent in every molecule, in every person, in every*thing*, then that makes a difference to our understanding of the Lord's Supper. We believe that we are consuming Him in a literal way, even though we cannot perceive Him with our physical senses. In faith, we believe that the bread and the wine are both radiant with the presence of Christ.

There's a danger of losing the practical understanding and indulging in philosophy here, and that's not at all my intention. Rather, I would emphasize that the reason for including this section is to strengthen our faith, and to reinforce that our lives are indeed hidden in Christ and united with Him.

Whether we believe we are consuming Christ metaphorically or literally, the most important thing is how it impacts our faith. For some, the understanding that the Spirit of Christ is indeed omnipresent can help greatly. However, even if our approach *is* literal, we still need to use God's gift of imagination to bring life to what we believe. Imagination and metaphor are absolutely vital in the life of faith and prayer. We don't have to believe that we are literally consuming the Christ in order for our faith to be ignited, and for the power of the symbolism of the Lord's Supper to be active in our experience. It is the activity of faith that counts. Jesus said, "According to your faith and trust and reliance [on the power invested in Me] be it done to you" (Matt. 9:29, AMPC).

WHAT DOES IT MEAN TO BE ONE WITH CHRIST AND RAISED WITH HIM?

It means much more than can ever be expressed in a book, or even a trillion books. However, we can at least start by looking at the implications of the truth that we have already been raised with Christ and that our life is fully integrated with His: "You died, and your life is hidden with Christ in God" (Col. 3:3).

It is significant that the New Testament refers to our being "in Christ" at least 160 times. These references also include slightly different expressions such as "in Him" and "in the Lord," but the meaning is the same. Knowing and actively resting in our position and identity in Christ is vitally important, if we desire to see the power of God released within us and through us.

It means that, in Spirit, we have been set free from the limitations of our finite, mortal bodies and are now spiritual beings. We are fully united with Christ: "the person who is joined to the Lord is one spirit with him" (1 Cor. 6:17, NLT). A completely new kind of life is now available to us: "We were dead and buried with him in baptism, so that just as he was raised from the dead by that splendid Revelation of the Father's power so we too might rise to life on a new plane altogether" (Rom. 6:4, PHILLIPS). On that "new plane" we are joint heirs with Christ (Rom. 8:17) and now share in His infinity, His immortality, His purity, His righteousness, and His overcoming. We have the very DNA of Christ operating in every cell of our beings, and we have His blood flowing in our arteries, veins, and capillaries—the blood that overcame the world, that burns up every trace of sin and that imparts the very life of God wherever it flows.

We have all this at the level of Spirit. Spirit is our true nature, and our three-dimensional bodies are a part of it—not the other way round. The problem is that, for more than two thousand years, there has been a tendency to place an enormous, unbalanced emphasis on our limited, physical bodies, and the true gospel has been distorted in order to make it fit with human philosophy. This has been at the cost of stifling the immeasurable power that God has made available to us—if we would but believe His word and act upon it.

"Christ in you, the hope of glory" (Col. 1:27) is often quoted but it can only be understood in terms of infinite Spirit. How can Christ—who has all the attributes of omnipotent and omnipresent God—be contained within a human body? The "you" in this verse must refer to the "you" that is infinite Spirit, the adopted son or daughter, made one with the Father.

We are told that the Holy Spirit lives within us: "Do you not know that you are the temple of God and that the Spirit of God dwells in you?" (1 Cor. 3:16). This is a most glorious truth but, again, it points to infinite Spirit. Wherever the Spirit of God is, He is there in all His fulness—He cannot be divided.

In John 17:23, Jesus clearly says, "I in them, and You in Me." Paul expands upon that truth in his letter to the Ephesian church: "There is one body and one Spirit . . . one God and Father of all who is over all and through all and in all" (Eph. 4:4, 6) and Paul also declares: "In Christ you too are filled with the Godhead—Father, Son and Holy Spirit—and reach full spiritual stature" (Col. 2:10, AMPC).

Current scientific knowledge strongly reinforces and sheds light on these—and many other—scriptures and spiritual truths that have, for centuries, been considered largely as metaphors. The time has come to see that they are much more than metaphor. In fact, these truths are waiting to be fanned into flame by the faith of believers. Then, along with St. Augustine, we will be able to say, "Faith is to believe what you do not see; the reward of this faith is to see what you believe."

To continue to think of ourselves as individuals living separate and apart from God not only hinders the flow of spiritual power in our lives but it can also be a form of pride: a wilful rebellion against the scriptural revelation of the Holy One. Let us hold fast, therefore, to the truth that because of Calvary there is no more separation; we are fully united with the Godhead. Let us align ourselves with the "tremendous . . . power available to us who believe in God" (Eph. 1:19, PHILLIPS) and see it begin to pour out, healing and transforming as it flows.

"Now to Him who is able to do exceedingly abundantly above all that we ask or think, according to the power that works in us, to Him be glory in the church by Christ Jesus to all generations, forever and ever. Amen" (Eph. 3:20–21).